MW01493225

EVERY ROOM TELLS A STORY

TALES FROM THE PAGES OF nest MAGAZINE

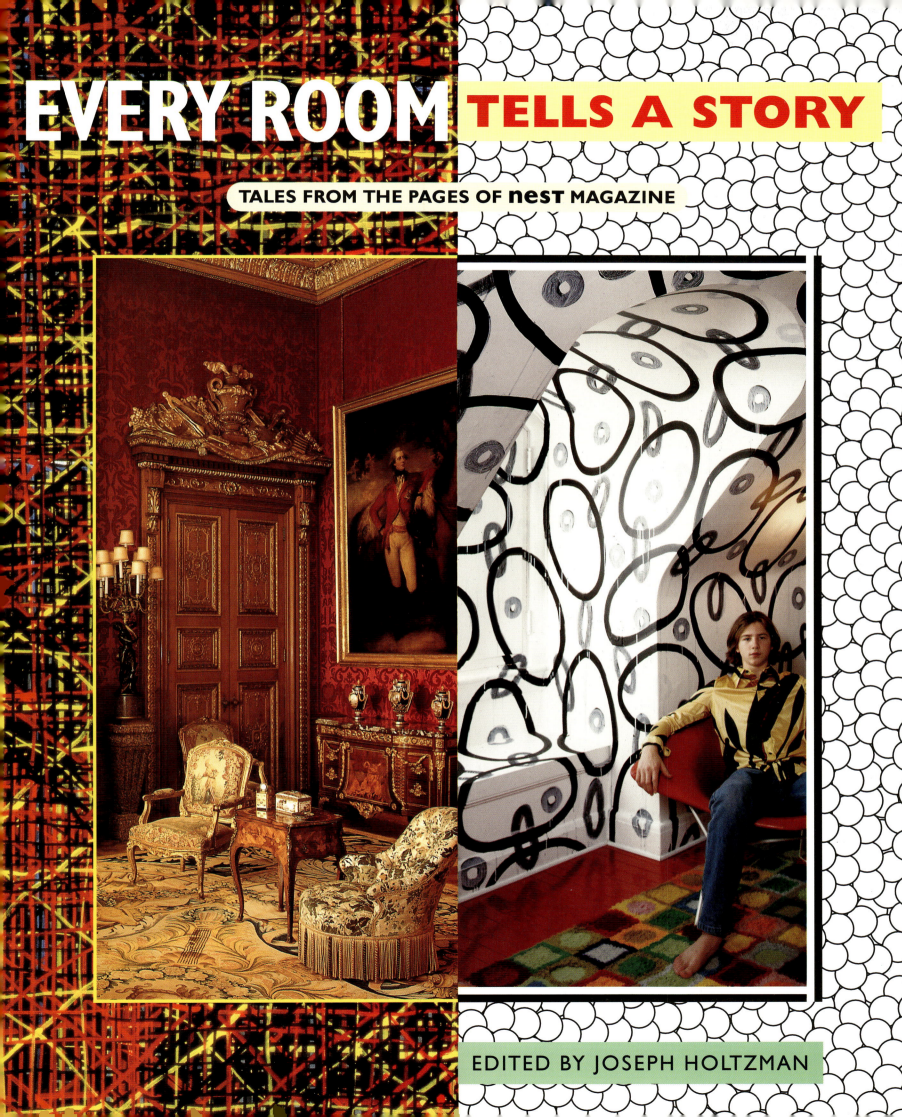

EDITED BY JOSEPH HOLTZMAN

About the jacket: The jacket on this book is the one element that was not designed by **nest**! With the good-humored blessing of our publisher, D.A.P., we reproduce our original cover proposal on the previous page. In their own words, D.A.P.'s marketing and sales people "thought the book needed a jacket to clothe and protect it in the sometimes inhospitable climate of the marketplace, before the magical moment when the book comes home to roost in the hands of a loving reader."

EVERY ROOM TELLS A STORY

TALES FROM THE PAGES OF nest MAGAZINE

EDITED BY   *Joseph Holtzman*
JOSEPH HOLTZMAN

INTRODUCTION BY   MATTHEW STADLER

TEXT BY   CARL SKOGGARD

D.A.P./Distributed Art Publishers, Inc. New York

Published by D.A.P./Distributed Art Publishers, Inc.
155 Sixth Avenue
New York, NY 10013
Tel: (212) 627-1999   Fax: (212) 627-9484

© 2001 **nest** Books LLC
1365 York Avenue
New York, NY 10021

Cover: Skuta Helgason and Craig Willis for D.A.P.
Cover photographs: Doug Brown, Derry Moore, and Antoine Bootz

Introduction copyright © 2001 Matthew Stadler
Text copyright © 2001 Carl Skoggard

Managing editor and copy editor: Paul B. Franklin
Production manager: Della R. Mancuso
Graphics directors: Charlotte Whalen and Tom Beckham
Typography: Jennifer Dossin
Chief financial officer for **nest** Books LLC: Patricia Stacom

Printed and bound in Milan, Italy, by
Arti Grafiche Amilcare Pizzi, s.p.a.
ISBN 1-891024-28-0

INTRODUCTION

nest is headquartered in the spare room of an apartment on Manhattan's Upper East Side. The office is largely taken up with books, stacked floor to ceiling on steel shelves, scattered machinery, a few desks, and boxes of magazines. If the entire staff of ten ever came to work on the same day, half of us would have to stand. But that will never happen; the managing editor lives in Paris, the literary editor, me, in Portland, Oregon, and the copy editor has never set foot in the building. **nest**'s founder and editor-in-chief, Joseph Holtzman, shows up every day (it's his apartment), and one can usually find Joe's assistant, Steven Varni, and chief financial officer, Pat Stacom, at their desks, trying to translate one of Joe's ideas—10,000 bees in a downtown studio for a Napoleonic reliquary; 400 pounds of gingerbread for wallpapering a bedroom; edible paper for a story on kitchens—into a viable set of plans. This room is home to a charming, sometimes charmed, dialogue: impulse answered by elaboration, elaboration reined into reality—the impossible methodically plotted into a strategy of marvelous possibilities.

The first time I showed up, in April of 1997, there was no **nest**, and I had never met Joe. I am a novelist, not well known, and at that time I had three out-of-print novels and a job writing book reviews for a weekly newspaper in Seattle. Someone (it was Kiera Coffee) called me from New York asking would I like to write about Keith Haring's men's-room wall murals for a magazine called **nest**. I was just vain enough to be entirely unsurprised by the call. "Of course," I told her, "I'd love to. And what exactly is **nest**?" Hiring unknown-

novelists to write about public toilets was fairly typical of the early **nest** strategy. More typical, when I sent in the requested two hundred words (eleven of which turned out to be "dick") Joe read them and flew me to New York to ask would I like to be the editor of his magazine. That is how we met. At **nest**, merit is rewarded without hesitation, sometimes without merit.

In the spare room, at that time, Joe had assembled a group of friends, some well-suited to magazine work, others disastrously not, and saddled them with a list of two dozen stories plus a late July deadline. **nest** was Joe's answer to the imprecations of a friend, Aiden Shaw, who had told Joe to please stop complaining about lousy shelter magazines and just make a better one. (Issue 1 credits Aiden on the masthead: He is listed as "Kick-In-The-Ass.") A slave to craftsmanship, Joe wanted the Milan art-book printer Amilcare Pizzi to produce **nest**, so press time had already been booked; the erstwhile staff had three months to get the issue ready. By "editor," I soon discovered, Joe meant he wanted someone to deal with all the text ("the gray stuff," as he still calls it). "I don't read," he lied. "So just hire whoever you really admire. As long as you love the texts we'll publish them." To this generous offer I eventually said "yes." And so **nest** has functioned for the four years since. Anything visual Joe deals with; all the words are my business. I like to think Joe's instincts are good. The short history of the magazine suggests they are.

While Joe had never made a magazine before, he has been a decorator all his life. He's practiced on his own rooms since age five—when his choice at Moore's Toy Barn was a miniature sofa (maple colonial with ruffled seat cushions)—and spent the last decade arranging the houses of clients in Baltimore and New York. In his spare time he re-hangs museums and galleries, though mostly in his head. The shift from rooms to magazines may not be an obvious one, but Joe's preoccupations have lent themselves well to it: He is obsessed with surface and color. Looking at his apartment (as readers of **nest** can do in issue 2: "Yes, I too married a decorator . . .") one can't help but suspect that Joe feels constrained by the appalling finitude of surfaces indoors. On one wall of his dining room he had Pat O'Brien paint interlocking circles over stripes to multiply its meager two dimensions into many; meanwhile, in the main room, Pat applied tens of thousands of tiny pencil marks, by hand, floating over broad white and aqua stripes to transform the flat walls (and ceiling) into something much more expansive. My mother was nauseated by the photos of these rooms, literally; they gave her a kind of vertigo. While the square footage inside **nest** is, by comparison, miserably small, the number of pages must have been intoxicating. Nearly two hundred fresh new surfaces per issue.

Joe is somewhat of a stranger to new technologies, so he relies on his "computer prostheses," Tom Beckham and Charlotte Whalen, to realize the design of **nest**. Under Joe's direction, Tom and Charlotte manhandle the powerful machines, rearranging the multitude of parts that go into the magazine. Texts come flowing in from my side and film gets messengered from around the globe, all in preparation for the critical week in Milan: the production of the next issue at Pizzi.

As **nest** readers know, lavish production is a hallmark of the magazine. We have done nearly everything one can do to bound pages: punctured them, sliced them, burned and cut-and-pasted them; applied flocked wallpapers and scratch-and-sniff patches; enclosed punch-out cardboard models and vinyl Colorforms; perforated, ribboned, and girdled whole issues. None

of these acrobatics would have been possible without Della Mancuso, **nest**'s production manager and chief diplomat. Her skills in both fields (now aided by managing editor Paul Franklin) have been crucial to the magazine's survival and, really, its opulence. While Della's tenure has stretched from the early days until now, other important members of the **nest** staff have come and gone: Sean Brennan, James Spagnoletti, Wouter Dolk, Allegra Peyton, Ingred Castro, Alex Castro, Sarah Myers, Margaret Pinette, and Laura Morris.

nest was not the untenanted playground Joe had promised me. It came with some writers attached, and this was very fortunate indeed. Among these were two who would form the voice and style of the magazine more profoundly than any others: Lisa Zeiger and Carl Skoggard. If **nest** has a consistent voice at all, it is largely carried in the unattributed texts—the captions, tables of contents, and occasional forays into design history—provided by the staff writer (Lisa for the first six issues, and Carl more or less since then). They play host to the virtual party each issue is conceived as being. Carl's dry wit and almost embarrassing mastery of obsolete slang always lend a reassuring tone to what might otherwise be a too dizzying journey through the dozens of themes taken on by our customary Whitman's sampler of writers. Just as a first-class seamstress relies on her thread-maker to keep quality consistent, we lean on Carl to provide a voice that can stitch each issue together.

Every ingredient of the magazine is scrutinized. Photographers, writers, paper stock, typefaces, colors, inks, even the shape of each issue—every choice is painstaking and deliberate. When the glued binding of issue 1 fell apart we immediately switched to an expensive sewn binding, then even went back to print a new run using the better method. America's last extant flocking factory was engaged to produce Rosemarie Trockel's specially commissioned wallpaper for issue 2; Italian paper wizard Jesus Moctezuma was brought in to design the carefully laid out parts of our cardboard punch-out recreation of Goya's Quinta del Sordo; Todd Oldham designed original scratch-off swimwear for our nude cover models in issue 9. We choose collaborators as carefully as Joe would his wall fabrics.

Inevitably, a magazine's collaborators include advertisers. Most magazines are, in fact, designed principally by their advertisers; that is, ads take up more than half their pages. At **nest** we restrict them to a third or less (so Joe will always be our principal designer), but we're nevertheless fascinated by ads. We ask all our advertisers to consider each issue's unique formatting (die-cuts, punched holes, laser burns, what-have-you) as they design for us. Further, we never hesitate to involve them in thought-provoking juxtapositions as we lay out the "ad well." Prada's exquisitely clothed models looked especially bound and posed in issue 9 when we ran them opposite a placid nude couple in an indoor Garden of Eden we'd commissioned from landscape architect Ken Smith. While our "editorial well" runs uninterrupted by paid ads, that hasn't kept us from using advertising and its remarkable design history as fodder for an article or two. A faux marketing campaign for Tom Sach's **nest**-commissioned *Bitch Lounge* ran in issue 7 and nearly got us disqualified for a national magazine award. Luckily, no customers ever called to buy one, and the award committee believed our claim that this wasn't a "real ad" so much as a comment on ads. A third of what we put into the world with each issue is advertising, so we've tried to make that an explicit part of the conversation.

nest is essentially an ongoing conversation rendered in print. Most magazines are. In our case, this fact is reinforced by an editorial process solely comprised of talking about stories and then pursuing them. If what I care about is hard-core punk rock then, yes, I should go ahead and write about mosh pits as instances of interior decoration. If someone (more than one) on staff smokes a lot of dope, why not commission the design of

marijuana chintz? And how about a gardening piece on an indoor pot garden? Denmark? Scotland? By all means, go. I'm still at work on my exposé of the Brazilian soccer team's locker room. Apparently they have eleven matching bathtubs, all in a row, for the starting players, plus eleven daybeds. Too bad for you if you're a sub.

To the extent that we concern ourselves at all with the interests of our readers, we are concerned simply with their apprehension of beauty, rather than, say, with their habits as consumers. We try to catalyze our readers' apprehension of beauty in a broad range of things and circumstances. We expose them to interiors where they do not normally look for beauty—prisons, igloos, kids' bedrooms, birds' nests, the bathroom, a cardboard box for the homeless—and help them see. By balancing these unlikely subjects with the more traditional fodder of interiors magazines (the homes of the wealthy or famous), we've managed to keep **nest** focused on beauty rather than the feeding of consumer interests. I'm very glad we have.

Writing novels was excellent preparation for my work at **nest**. My time is largely spent looking at sentences, thinking about the ways text can be elegant and meaningful and not go stale. If you find this hackneyed or unbelievable, I couldn't agree with you more. After four years of it, I still feel stabs of suspicion whenever Joe says to me, for example, "A poem? Why not, if you really like the poet." Am I being set up? Is the long rope of my dull-headed lack of taste being strung out—in lavish four-color pages distributed worldwide—simply to hang me? If so, here I hang—here the entire **nest** staff hangs—with no screen of marketing, demographic surveys, nor ulterior motives to mask the plain appearance of our tastes and curiosities in the world. To do this kind of thing at all well is a peculiar, even private, accomplishment. I am astonished, and grateful, that it matters to anyone.

Matthew Stadler

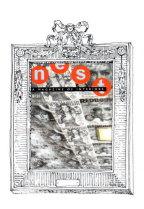

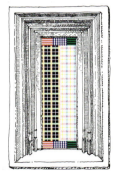

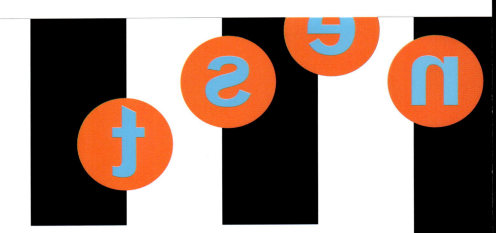

WAIST NOT, WANT NOT

As anyone who has ever tried it knows, to create means to begin—again and again. Still, there is something special about beginning for the first time. And how did we begin the premier issue of **nest**, which had its newsstand release late in November 1997?

With a hundred or more images of Farrah Fawcett-Majors on our front cover, or to be more precise, with a collage of other magazine covers with her on them. The magazine start-up consultant had said: "Now you mustn't ever, *ever* show other magazines this way! Subliminal advertising for them, you see." The magazine consultant knew we were making a huge mistake. But if any **nest** cover was wildly successful, this was it.

The cover story told how ex-altar boy Raymond Donahue had turned his mother's suburban New Jersey attic into a rigorously elegant shrine to Farrah. It went to our hearts. As **nest** editor-in-chief Joseph Holtzman observed in his first letter to readers: "Some of us discover ourselves by bringing many an odd thing indoors over a lifetime. For others, home is a single truth always known, the drumbeat of obsession."

In the letter our editor-in-chief also warned readers that **nest** houses have "private parts," that the magazine had no plans to be a "waist-up publication." Here the premier issue delivered abundantly, with several waist-down features. Lord Bath's private suite at Longleat, one of England's greatest Tudor homes, disclosed a cosmos of his own inventing that was part Blake, part Kamasutra ("Plastic Fantastic Lover"). And we went on to document Keith Haring's brave, wriggly sex murals in the second-floor men's room of New York's Lesbian and Gay Community Services Center (Matthew Stadler, the writer for this piece, came up with its title: "Haring's Guernica").

There was more audacity in Holtzman's pledge that **nest** would show readers what they had "not seen before—perhaps not even imagined." For one does see and imagine a lot these days—though probably nothing like Raymond's attic shrine or Lord Bath's errant wall décor. But with the feature "Adam's Rooms" **nest** did take things one step further, creating an eye-popping bedroom suite from scratch for a 15-year-old boy—a starkly original place no one could have seen before.

Opposite page: The FFM cover shows ceiling and walls of Raymond Donahue's attic bedroom, expertly papered with homemade photocopied multiples of magazine covers featuring his idol. For the surface of this cover, spot varnish was applied to the **nest** logo and the oversized television screen; remaining areas used a matte finish. *This page:* The rear cover, in bold stripes, was glossy but did not carry an ad. From the beginning **nest** has kept to advertising policies that set it apart from other magazines.

Cover photograph Jason Schmidt

Photographs Jason Schmidt and original text Valerie Steele

nest

Dear Reader

"What is human?" Are we little lower than the angels or merely poor, bare, forked creatures? However elusive the answer, part of it is always found in our houses.

nest offers its own definitions in celebrating human self-invention at home. As many as are the ways of domesticity, our photographers and writers reveal them in a spirit of fun and, occasionally, daring.

nest wants to be read by anyone who wakes up in the morning or in the afternoon with healthy curiosity about how others express themselves where they live. We hope to show you things you've not seen before—perhaps not even imagined, as well as shed our own light on some familiar places. And, reader, be advised: our houses have private parts. **nest** is no waist-up publication.

Of course we are equally fascinated by home-making psychology. You know how mysterious it can get. Some of us discover ourselves by bringing many an odd thing indoors over a lifetime. For others, home is a single truth always known, the drumbeat of obsession, a place built against outside. (When need arises, **nest** resorts to the couch.)

Finally, reader, be assured: our focus will never be on focus groups. We'd love an authentic chunk of your mind, though. Comments and also suggestions for features are always welcome.

5

Opposite page: Another view of Raymond Donahue's room with Farrah herself, or almost, lying in wait. And here is the collector himself as he appeared at his first communion in 1973 and, later, with stigmata (his neck tattoo being the bar code from Farrah Shampoo by Fabergé). We also showed the exterior of the Donahue residence in New Jersey. **nest** takes little interest in the outside of inside, but who could resist the perfection of Raymond's façade? *Above:* The earliest letter from our editor-in-chief set out the philosophy behind **nest**. It continues to be a favorite source for puzzled journalists trying to explain us to the world.

Joseph Holtzman

6

The exterior of Longleat, Lord Bath's magnificent seat in greenest Wiltshire. Readers needed this view to fully comprehend the heresy being perpetrated within these ancient walls. Images for "Plastic Fantastic Lover" were shot by Derry Moore, the most distinguished of all photographers of English country homes (and nest's London editor).

TEXT MITCHELL OWENS   PHOTOGRAPHS DERRY MOORE

PLASTIC FANTASTIC LOVER

Longleat was built in 1568 by Sir John Thynne, assisted by master country-house architect Robert Smythson and a Frenchman, Allen Maynard. The house's external form evinces the classical symmetry of the Renaissance, while towering mullioned windows resurrect the medieval Perpendicular style. *Overlaid, at left:* a detail from a Canaletto etching of Padua, ca. 1741.

8

Lord Bath and best friend posed in a private drawing room at Longleat. Its sprawling third floor has been
fairly covered with his crusty murals, kneaded in a custom mix of oil, paint, and sawdust.
Opposite page: The original 16th-century circular stairs provide gallery space
for portraits Lord Bath has made of his mistresses (including one-night stands). When we paid our call,
there were 64 of these hanging. Hereabouts his lordship is called the Loins of Longleat.

Three figures from Lord Bath's Kamasutra murals—a "glorious cornucopia of goggle-eyed copulatory bliss" according to the hardworking artist.
A suitable frame for the image came from a detail of William Blake's *Whirlwind of Lovers* (an illustration for Dante's *The Divine Comedy*). **nest** has always been as interested in frames as in pictures.
Opposite page: Toilet stalls, solemn as choir stalls, beneath Keith Haring's mural in the New York Lesbian and Gay Community Services Center. Here is a room where "mourning is celebration," as Matthew Stadler, our writer, put it.

Photograph Jan Groover

Two rooms designed in 1997 by **nest** editor-in-chief Joseph Holtzman for Adam Gidwitz of Baltimore, as realized by painter Patrick O'Brien. The way patterns in the Day Room and the Night Room riot over almost everything in sight would echo sooner or later in page layouts of the magazine. Fifteen-year-old Adam submitted his own description of these rooms, which we printed unedited.

12

Photographs Doug Brown

FALL 1998

nest

2

ne st

a quarterly magazine of INTERIORS $9.70

Flocked Wallpaper by Rosemarie Trockel see p. 124

FLOCKING AND FLUSHING

The only predictable thing about **nest**, its regular quarterly publication, began with our second issue (fall 1998). This time, though, the cover was actually many different covers. True, every single copy bore a hand-applied cutting of flocked wallpaper commissioned by **nest** from the German artist Rosemarie Trockel. The trouble was that we offered eight of her enigmatic shapes from which to choose—each its own hazy notion of some undiscovered continent. (Collectors of the magazine, take note.)

The cover also made **nest** an object to be knowingly touched. Its alternating matte and gloss background stripes and the two levels of felt on each Trockel wallpaper sample meant that four distinct sensations could be had by running your finger over the surface. We were offering readers a cunning and mysterious object, not a quick read. Perhaps (we hoped) you would hesitate to throw it away. Those who did anyway tossed out $5.50 at a minimum reckoning (our investment in paper and printing per copy).

Signaling **nest**'s commitment to blue-chip decorating with a twist, "Tall and Well Stacked" revealed the 9 levels of a miniature Flatiron Building in downtown Turin converted to a private house—so many flights of fancy for the great Renzo Mongiardino, whose favorite project this was. Not long before, the Italian interior designer had actually had the live-in folly reproduced in marzipan cake to celebrate his 80th birthday.

Home style and anthropology are often made to cross paths in **nest**. "Igloo" commemorated a vanishing shelter form and, as always, took readers inside. Rare photos of the interiors of Inuit snow houses from 50 years ago were provided by Richard Harrington, one of the world's great documentary photographers, who shared as well his own recollection of igloo living.

Again and again, **nest** returns to the question of advertising, what it does and how. "Hasi Hester" reran a series of ads from the early 1980s. These had been staged and shot by an actor turned decorator and textile designer, to market his mad fabric fashions. Hasi, the main prop in all his own ads, seemed to us a most amusing Angeleno. Repositioned in the editorial well of **nest** 2, his ad pages readily yielded up their Hollywood-wannabe subtext. The brief accompanying narrative spoke of the real Hasi (a.k.a. Horace) Hester, a Pea Ridge, Kentucky, native endowed with spirit and grit.

Lest anyone forget for even a minute that houses have their private parts, **nest**'s editor-in-chief treated readers in this issue to a disquisition on bathroom etiquette by one of his favorite writers, Sophie Hadida, drawn from her once authoritative *Manners for Millions* (1932). Our feature, simply titled "The Bathroom," was illustrated with photographs and diagrams from a 1970s manual on bathroom engineering and design.

Finally, "A Room of One's Own" showed how four inmates in the New Mexico Women's Correctional Facility, near Grants, New Mexico, individualized their tiny standard-issue living spaces. Each decorator wrote her own accompanying text (**nest** having organized a writing class at the prison). This feature would receive considerable media attention; evidently many found the resourcefulness and dignity of the women moving.

Following two pages: An inside feature on Rosemarie Trockel ("Everything but the Chick") showed the new "Eiweiss" flocked paper hanging in her own guest bedroom where one could appreciate the play of its eight shapes and spacious diagonal repeats. Each shape originated as a smear of egg white. (The flocking process calls for powdered wool to be scattered on a surface to which glue or slow-drying varnish has been applied.)

Concerning slightly earlier events in this Zen-serene setting, Lisa Zeiger, our writer, testified: "In Cologne, in the winter of 1991, Love was colder than Death, and I was laid up in Trockel's unofficial hospital for broken hearts, a Guest Room reserved for girlfriends on the run from men in other cities, or in my case (and a case it was) another country. In my two-month stay, I used the Guest Room for both relapse and recovery, as heartbreak and hot-pillow hotel combined, repairing the lackadaisical sadism of a London capon with the ravishing cruelty of an Aryan alley cat who slunk in one night through the kitchenette window."

Igloo

Photographs and original text Richard Harrington

Previous two pages: Not all domes come from Rome, as those who perused our "Igloo" feature realized. Indeed, Inuit snow houses are the classic example of that supposed Western invention. Slabs of snow are first cut with a machete-like blade and shaved for precise fitting. The slabs, some eight inches thick and two by three feet in dimension, are then placed so they spiral upwards and inwards, very like a dome. "When the rounded key block at the top is in place the house is ready. It is so sturdy you can walk over it," wrote Richard Harrington.

Above: "Igloo" saw **nest** grazing on *National Geographic* terrain, but we kept our focus carefully domestic, taking pains to inform readers how and where all basic household—as well as purely bodily—functions would be carried out. The seasonal sojourning documented in this Harrington photo from the late 1940s is a thing of the past, though small igloos for overnight stops on the trail are still being built. Nostalgia pervades Harrington's own memory of living in one: "It was a unique time in my life. At times, all settled in our new igloo, full of food and warm tea, I would take one last step outside into the winter darkness. Our dog team had been fed and now all were curled head under tail. There is no moisture in the Arctic air. The stars and the moon gave enough light with reflection from the snowy ground. It was bright enough to read a paper—but who would if you could watch the majestic curtains woven by the aurora borealis? So silent I could hear my own heart thumping. And I thought there would not be another person in two or three hundred miles and without my companion's skill I would be dead within half an hour. And then we quietly crawled back into our igloo, drawing the snow lock into place and sealing us in for another night."

TALL

AND

WELL

STACKED

PHOTOGRAPHS
DERRY
MOORE
ORIGINAL TEXT
MITCHELL
OWENS

Above: Renzo Mongiardino's renderings of the footprint of the Gian Carlo Bussei house in Turin, and a cross-section of its 9 levels.

The double-story ground-floor dining room with built-in banquette seating (cross-section opposite), and the Roman bath at sub-basement level (cross-section below). In the former, a real waiter faces a dumbwaiter (concealed behind the right-hand cabinet). *Below:* Mongiardino stopped long enough to pose in the latter. To the right are glimpses of a curtained anteroom to the bath and the shower. *Following two pages:* Gian Carlo Bussei's private quarters, at the top of the house (cross-section above). Its walls are sheathed in white over damask, a double skin repeated on the floor with canvas over carpet. The fireplace valance was originally designed by Mongiardino for a Franco Zeffirelli film. In the adjoining bath, right, is a snug-fitting tub cloaked in gold mosaic; the walls are stenciled in gold on Ravenna blue.

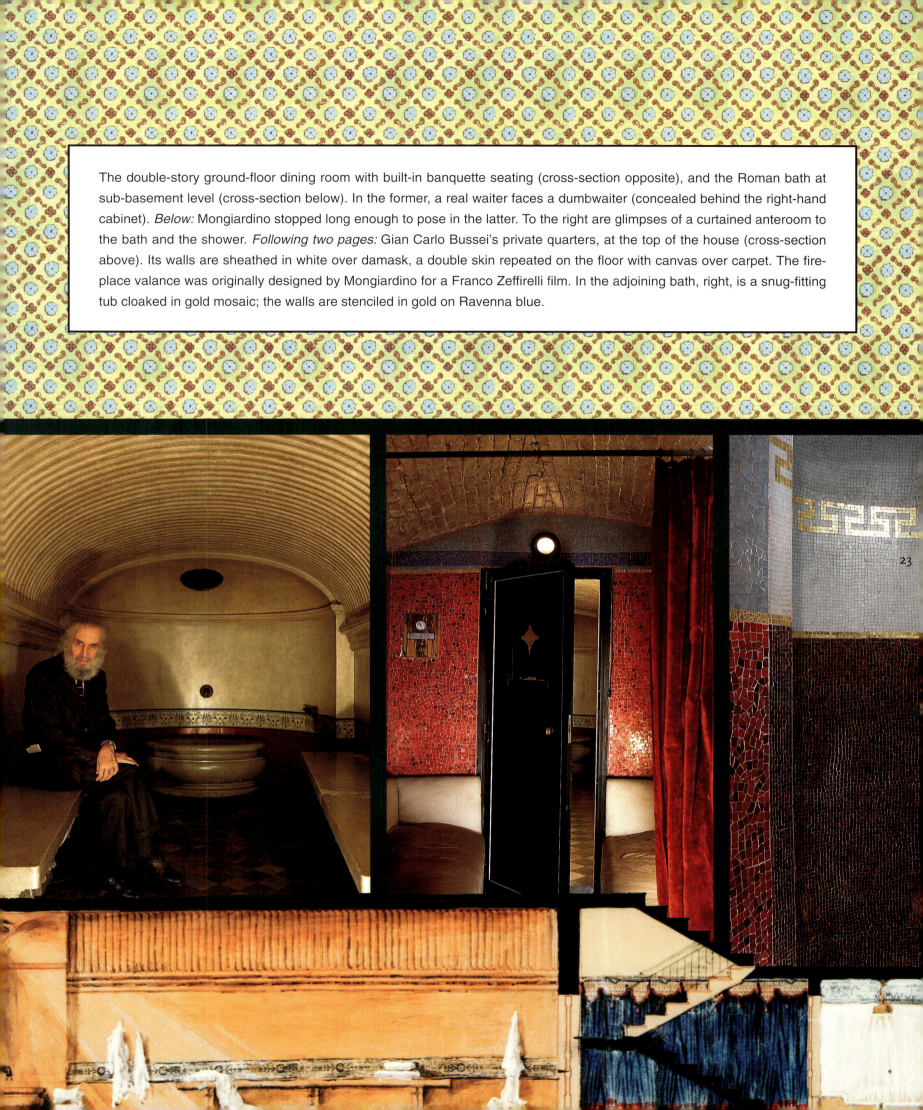

23

BED-SITS I HAVE KNOWN

—MURIEL SPARK—

A large part of my life, starting from war-time England, was taken up with bed-sitting rooms in London.

With the usual essentials and furnishings came the landlady or the housekeeper. She was part of the equipment; she had to be taken on, too. This included her life-story. I imagine it still does.

The room was furnished with a single, or if you were lucky, a three-quarter bed which you were expected never to share with anyone whomsoever, least of all a member of the opposite sex.

That settled, the next requirement was regular payment of the rent, with the accent on regular. A day or two's delay made the landlady nervous, and a request for a week's delay would result in a visible hardening of all her arteries, every one. If you were a woman you were expected to give a sympathetic ear to the landlady's story. This worked out at about fifteen minutes a day but if you were, for instance, a writer anxious to get on with your job, it seemed like an hour. On the other hand, as a novelist I found that these narrations were often very rewarding.

For men, I think the burden of daily chatter was less. On the whole landladies preferred their tenants to be out working all day. It took them time to get used to people working at home, but if you were seriously hard at it they became, in time, extremely supportive. In this I was lucky, and I still love to talk about, write about, my last landlady, Tiny Lazzari.

But first let me describe what the usual bed-sit comprised, along with the bed. Curtains and bed-covers frequently matched, and what were known as "autumn tints" generally prevailed. These yellows, golds, and bright browns were very much more liveable-with than the vivid stripes or spring-flower themes that were sometimes offered. The floorboards were either bare wood-stained and covered with rugs, or else linoleum. Either way the autumn reds and browns predominated on the floor-coverings. Surprisingly fine antique pieces of furniture could be found lying in wait in these bed-sits, among the otherwise mere junk. I remember a gate-legged table of extraordinary good quality; I remember a genuine Old Windsor chair and other treasures, in London's Ladbroke Grove and Holland Park (as well as the more advanced and slightly more expensive Clarges Street and Half-Moon Street of London W1). These last exclusive nests were preferred and frequented by the U.S. officers stationed in or passing through London during the final stages of World War II, that is, about 1943–45. Both in Clarges and in Half-Moon Streets, the rooms were larger and so were the cellars for which we all made a dive during air-raids, wearing the best-looking dressing gowns we could devise in those days of strict clothes rationing. The girlfriends of the U.S. officers were easily discerned from that point of view, being more glamourously clothed than all others. "Overpaid, over-sexed, and over here" was the verdict of our envious English enlisted men.

Half-Moon Street, by the way, is a perfectly straight byway between Piccadilly and Curzon Street. I wonder who lives there now? What are the furnishings like of this merry whoresville? In the war years the rooming houses in those exalted streets were not run by the usual widowed or somehow-single landlady, but by a definite couple who did all the serving of breakfasts, cleaning, and rent collecting. The rooms were more elegant than those in the outskirts and suburbs. There in the West End, you would never find stuffing oozing out a sofa-arm as you would in the friendlier, humbler Camberwell. There, the wallpaper tended to be pale green and white stripes, "the Regency Look." The bed was covered with beige and the curtains light gray.

Invariably, in all bed-sits there was a gas-ring with a meter into which one put shillings, or sometimes in the cheaper houses, pennies. This money was collected every month by the gas man who was reputed to be sexy. It was true they usually had some saucy remark. I remember:

"You got children, Ma'am?"

"Yes, but I'm not keen on a lot of children."

"No, but you like the other."

Today, I suppose, you could have them in court for less, but we just brushed it off in those hard-working but somehow care-free times.

The gas man always had a rebate, part of the collected money, to hand over. But this small offering never went into the pockets of the tenants. It had to be handed over to the landladies.

A sink or washbasin with hot and cold water taps was always provided in a corner of the room. The "h" and "c" on the taps seldom coincided with the promise of hot water. That depended on the hour of the day. Hot water was generally available from 7 o'clock to 9 in the morning and about the same hours in the evening. A bath could be obtained in the communal bath room and toilet on the landing. (Four pennies got a wonderful bath. For a shilling you could do a week's washing, a hair-wash, and a good bath.)

In the more expensive bed-sits, the floor-covering was beige wall-to-wall. The sofa and divan bed were dotted with large bright cushions which friends could use to sit on the floor. There was usually a sideboard with a cupboard in which you could keep drinks. A hanging cupboard for clothes and a chest of drawers were also supplied. But in one bed-sit in Kensington I was obliged to bring in an orange box where I kept my supplies of drinks and tea-making and lunch-snack provisions.

I haven't visited a bed-sit for many years, and often wonder if there has been much change. It was all so functional and basic that I would be surprised if they differ much now from those days of the 40s and 50s. In the 60s, when I went to work for a few years in New York, I stayed in a residential hotel on the East River. There I had virtually two rooms, a kitchen gallery with a city-gas stove, and my own bathroom. The management's policy was to give the tenant a choice of decoration, so that before I moved in I pored over samples of wallpaper and upholstery materials with the housekeeper. I was entitled to change the decor every six months but if anything I'd chosen began to get on my nerves they were willing to redecorate the rooms at any time. A maid brought me eight clean towels a day, four in the morning, four at night, and bed linen was changed every day. Meals could be wheeled in at any hour of the night or day. I paid a basic $450 a month plus a few trimmings, but I had never before basked in such luxury as I did in 1964–68 in the Beaux Arts Hotel on the East River, on the 14th floor overlooking the United Nations. I wrote two novels there, and a great many stories. Most days I would go over to the New Yorker building where the late editor William Shawn had given me an office to work in. This, too, I furnished to my taste (an indigo-blue carpet, a turquoise divan).

In the Beaux Arts residence, my first choices were a mustard-colored wall-to-wall carpeting with turquoise-blue upholstery, white walls, and curtains white with large yellow flowers. Maybe this sounds awful but it looked a dream. My second choice was less successful. I got the idea of one black armchair, the others colored with blue-flowered curtains. Not a success. I had it all changed into something more neutral, more anonymous. My friends preferred those peaceful schemes and so did I.

By the time I'd left the United States for a permanent home in Italy, I was ready to take on regular apartments and make a real home. But my bed-sit days were fine and fruitful. I will never forget them.

Nor will I ever forget Tiny Lazzari. She was Irish by birth, and when I met her in 1955 she was aged 66. I was then in the middle of my first novel, *The Comforters*. She rented rooms in her house at Camberwell, South London. I had an attic. She was protective, motherly, and sympathetic. She insisted that I eat a square meal, sharing her lunch for a minimal recompense (about 20 cents). I stayed for ten years. Later, when I was comparatively successful, we went to Paris together, her first trip abroad, where she bought a voluminous hat and some presents which she smuggled back to England, neatly tucked into that hat. She protected me on the phone and at the front gate from intruders. Hers had been the best bed-sitter any hard-up working author could wish for. When I left it was a real wrench. Tiny lived until she was ninety-eight, still active and neat with pretty blue eyes. She died of old age, nothing more.

Hasi Hester

Hasi Hester

ORIGINAL TEXT   VINCENT FECTEAU AND MICHAEL LOBEL

These days many fashion and decorating magazines are a mix of ads and faux editorial features that scarcely bother to disguise their advertising purpose. "Hasi Hester" let **nest** poke a little fun at this dubious state of affairs. What looks for all the world like a series of ads is really a story about ads—and a man. Years before (our text disclosed), Hester had been in a fiery car wreck that killed his close friend, the actor Dirk Rambo. Among other things, the images advertise burn scars on the back of Hester's hands.

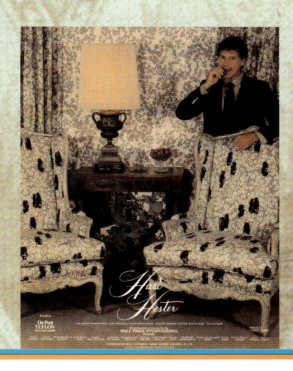

When it appeared in **nest** 2, this heat-seeking Diesel ad caused an outcry. We should have known better than to think that anything can be turned into a joke. After all, a fashion ad making light of the Holocaust or slavery would be unthinkable. So why did butchered female mannequins not set off our alarm bells? The expressions of dismay and outrage from so many readers, male and female, were sobering. The ad never appeared in any other American magazine (Europeans felt no similar qualms). We show it here in owning up to one of our bigger mistakes.

A ROOM OF ONE'S OWN

Photographs
Marcel Bardon and Albrecht Fuchs
Original text
Kiera Coffee

Barbara Phillips's cell in the New Mexico Women's Correctional Facility, near Grants, New Mexico. She sewed and crocheted covers in green and gold for every surface she could. In issue 2, **nest** readers were also shown the same space but bare, with the built-ins exposed: a stainless steel sink and toilet, desk and seat bolted to the wall, and bunk suspended between triangular brackets. Inmates' written statements for **nest** made mention of a "cell," "living quarters," or at most, "my room." Only one used the word "home."

Barbara Phillips

I was taught as a child to make do with what you have until you can make it better and from the reality of the reminder of my view to the spun fantasy of an orderly room I maintain a balance between what is and isn't, what can and can't be. With any station in life it would be nice to have more living space. I could stand to have a bigger cabinet with drawers to store items in, instead of having to bag everything and put it under the bed. At times my room seems cluttered and at other times too spacious, but with more room to store things it would feel that much more stable. I would like it if I could rearrange my room, such as moving my bed away from the cold wall, especially now that it's wintertime. Doing my cell took a lot of hard painstaking work. I crocheted a blanket, doilies for my table, seat, locker and footlocker, made picture frames, a tape box, vases, etc. I sewed and resewed pillows and bed skirts and ultimately found the intended effects forming. There isn't much room and at times the limit of what's appropriate for a cell crosses my mind, but never hinders my creativity. It's a nice feeling to come into my room and feel good about my living quarters. Being able to have my room as I like it, an image of my certain tastes, my own ideas put together by me, is a consolation in light of what the whole of prison life is about.

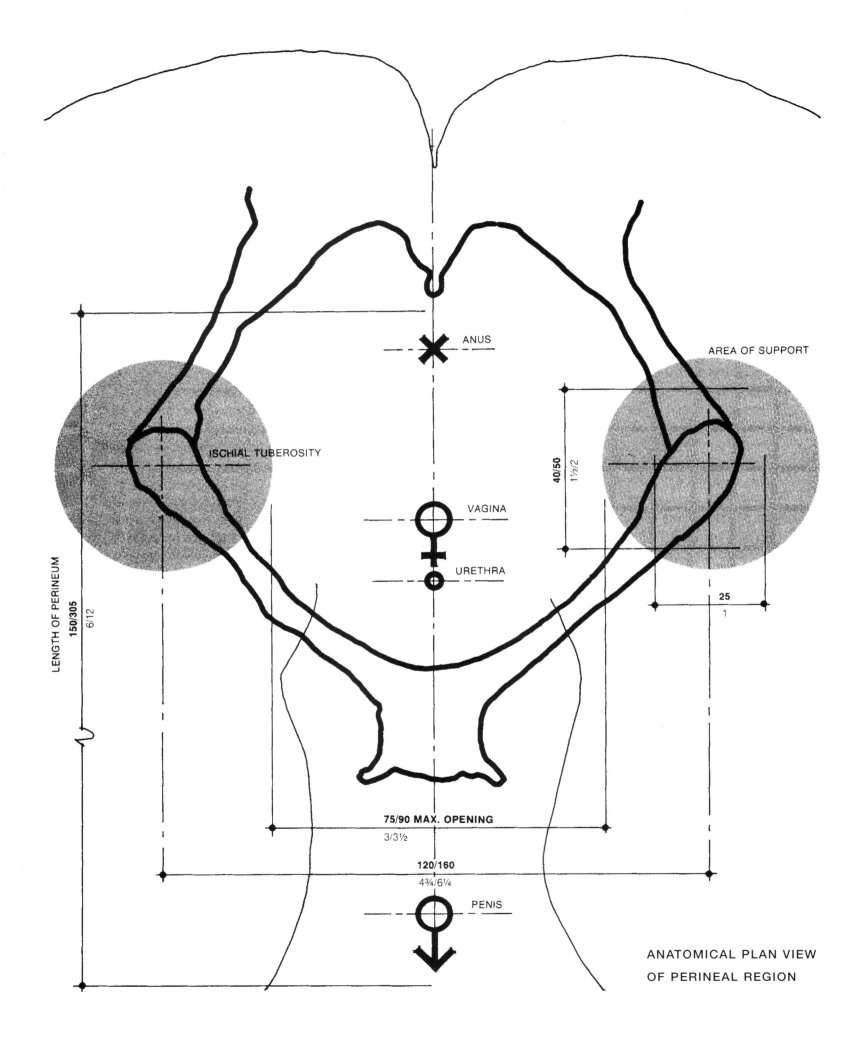

32

ANUS

AREA OF SUPPORT

ISCHIAL TUBEROSITY

VAGINA

40/50
1½/2

URETHRA

LENGTH OF PERINEUM
150/305
6/12

25
1

75/90 MAX. OPENING
3/3½

120/160
4¾/6¼

PENIS

ANATOMICAL PLAN VIEW
OF PERINEAL REGION

"WOHNBAD" OR "LIVING BATH": RÖHM, DARMSTADT, WEST GERMANY

Opposite page: In "The Bathroom" nesт wanted its readers to see things from the bottom up. An especially diverting diagram was taken from Alexander Kira's *The Bathroom: New and Expanded Edition,* 1976. Based on seven years of research at Cornell University, Kira's tome set its sights on "the most important private place in the house, and unquestionably the most badly designed." *Above:* This photo, also from Kira, illustrates a 1960s open-form living area centered on the bathroom, shared by the whole family as a part of daily living. Kira argued for the bathroom as a part of social space historically— citing not Louis XIV as might have been expected, but Elsie de Wolfe, who entertained friends there. *Following two pages:* In using Kira's documentation of male urination, nesт went not only graphic but with the flow, and quite possibly hinted its opinion re Miss Hadida's pronouncements. While Kira, warming to the topic, provided this anecdote in science's name: "Two drunken Russians are urinating out-of-doors one cold winter night. Petrov, swaying, says to his companion, 'Tell me, Ivan Ivanovich, why is it that when I piss it is like the snow falling silently on the white breast of Mother Russia, while when you piss it sounds like the roar of our mighty river Volga?' 'Because, Comrade Petrov, you are pissing on my fur coat.'"

Original text Sophie C. Hadida, 1932
PHOTOGRAPHS AND DIAGRAMS
FROM *THE BATHROOM*, 1976

THE BATHR●●M

in every home should be spotless. There are four objects in it that need the most painstaking care: the wash bowl, the tub, the toilet seat, and the flushbowl.

You may not believe it but there are many homes in which the tub is never cleaned after the bath. The person takes his bath, gets out,

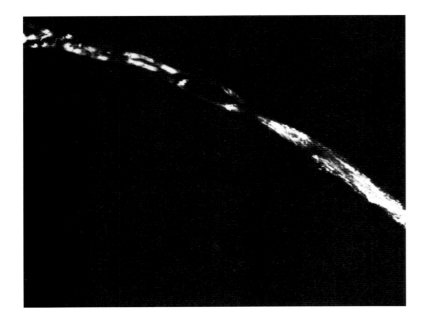

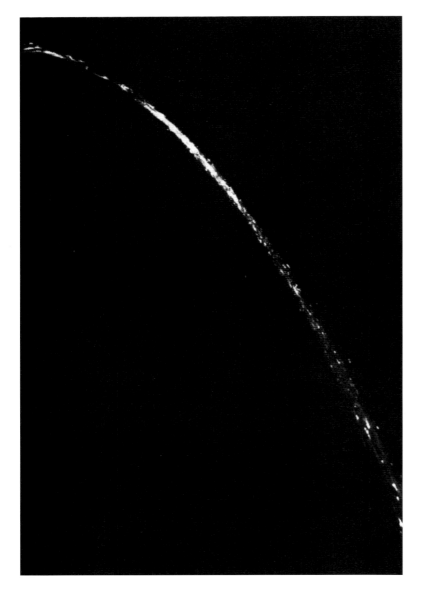

dresses, and walks out, leaving the tub for his mother or some other person to clean.

Every mother should train her family to take care of the tub immediately upon getting out. It is not a difficult task to wash the smooth surface before the deposit from the water and the soap has set, and such a task is not repugnant to the bather. But to leave it for anyone else is just disgusting, inconsiderate, and selfish; no person of any breeding would leave so menial a task for another.

A certain amount of cleaning should be done even where there is a maid, or in a hotel where one is paying well for that particular service. It takes but a moment to allow some clean water to flow in and out, and the maid may then finish without a sense of humiliation.

There are homes where the male members of the family consider this act beneath their dignity. They are deserving of little respect.

The washbowl, too, should be found spotlessly white as you enter the bathroom to use it. After you have finished, it is your task to see that it is clean and smooth, and that there is not the tiniest hair lying around. The soap should be rinsed; the soap dish, free from soapsuds; all personal

STREAM DISPERSION
CHARACTERISTICS OF MALE URINE STREAM

articles should be neatly put away: the toothbrush; the towels, folded or spread out smoothly on the towel rack to dry; the comb and brush, free from hair and otherwise clean, should be put away; and everything about the wash bowl should be left in a perfectly fresh and inviting condition. Pick up any hairpins that you have dropped. If all these things are neglected, never fail to remove the stopper from the bowl.

Towels that are soiled (but not damp) should be placed in the clothes basket found in most bathrooms; but if there is no basket, they should be neatly and inconspicuously placed all together for the maid, if there is one, to remove. Consideration for the service department in home or hotel is a mark of refinement. If there is no maid in the home, put the soiled towels where they belong. Never leave them for someone else (Cinderella) to take to the laundry.

After using the bathroom for any purpose whatsoever, open the window, whether in winter or summer, just for a few moments, out of consideration for the next person. Even after a steamy bath the air is most unpleasant, though perhaps not noticeably so to the occupant. It is considerate at special times to say, "Mary, don't go in for a few moments."

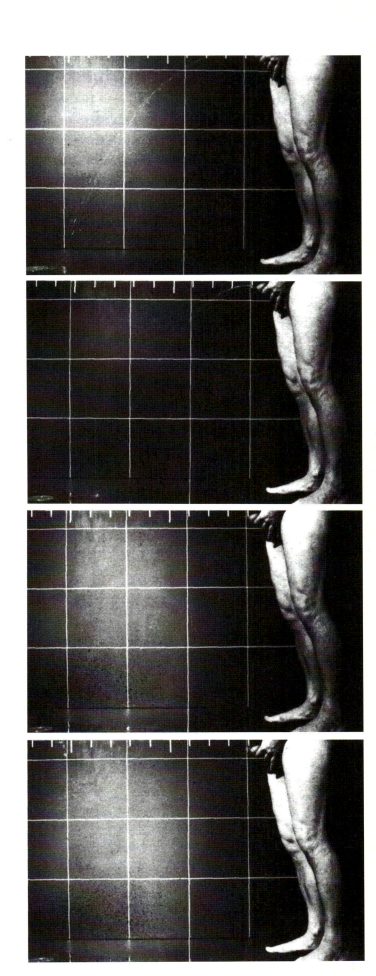

n
e
s
т

COMES BUT ONCE A YEAR

nest's first holiday issue (winter 1998-1999) was decked out as a surprise, in a three-and-three-quarter inch "belly band" commissioned from Todd Oldham. Each one of the 60,000 copies of the magazine had to be buttoned by hand. Of course, not only the fabric but also the quaint ogival button was an Oldham original. We, too, were surprised by this issue when production costs turned it into a fire-engine-red budget buster the likes of which we do not hope to see again.

At least there was no trouble with the newsstands or advertisers. That frontally nude woman on the cover was entirely concealed by the belly band until you undid the button. "Midnight Lace," our related feature, uncovered connections between a sternly sumptuous Carlo Mollino interior in Turin and the women he photographed there. It may be admitted: **nest** finds skin provocative (indoors only) and empty rooms merely provoking.

In his letter to readers, our editor-in-chief took aim at one of the most glaring aspects of room nudity—décor-starved ceilings. "Are we decorators or are we ostriches?" he thundered. "Face up to the Other Surface, I say." Anyone who takes a moment to reflect will share Holtzman's concern for interior decoration's stepchild and perhaps even forgive his off-the-wall rhetoric.

"Man of the Cloth," our feature on Todd Oldham's delicious fabric for **nest**, showed chairs in a 1928 period room at the Brooklyn Museum covered in the Pepto Teeter Totter colorways (jade, pine, and berry on zinnia pink). Most period rooms are aching to be dressed up a bit, don't you find? And, making sure we were well over-the-top with the Oldham business, **nest** inserted a generous double fold of Pepto Teeter Totter paper, presumably for readers to wrap a holiday gift in—say a few issues of their favorite magazine.

We also pulled out all the stops for our first major contemporary design feature. "Muleland" devoted 20 pages to the living/working space of designers Philip Agee and Stephen Penkowsky, hidden away just off San Francisco's Market Street. A full sequence of overall room shots and some two dozen vignettes were needed to document this extraordinary site of Bay Area creativity.

But **nest** 3 did not lack for bare shelters either. "Home Alone" led readers to ponder the mind of the Unabomber, Ted Kaczynski, while he holed up in his Montana cabin, and "Box of Rain" featured a high-design cardboard box created by a Dutchman for the homeless citizens of Rotterdam. Sometimes the most reduced interiors provide the richest food for thought, for inhabitants and the rest of us.

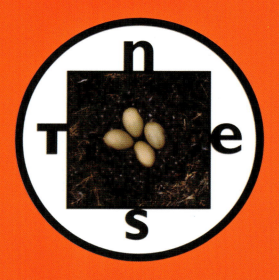

The Oldham belly band came in either cotton or polyester and in 14 limited-edition colorways, from Elf Mildew (mustard, beet, and kelly green on kiwi background) to Flips to Purple (berry, amber, and jade on periwinkle). Thinking of collectors, we made some varieties rarer than others: only 84 magazines were swathed in First Adobe Kiss (berry, orange, and cinnamon on dusty coral) whereas 8,129 copies got Sleeping Oriental (dirt, berry, and shrimp on persimmon). Incidentally, the original plan for this cover was to encrust it in red glitter, front and back. A tight publishing schedule made us change our mind; readers got only the red undercoat.

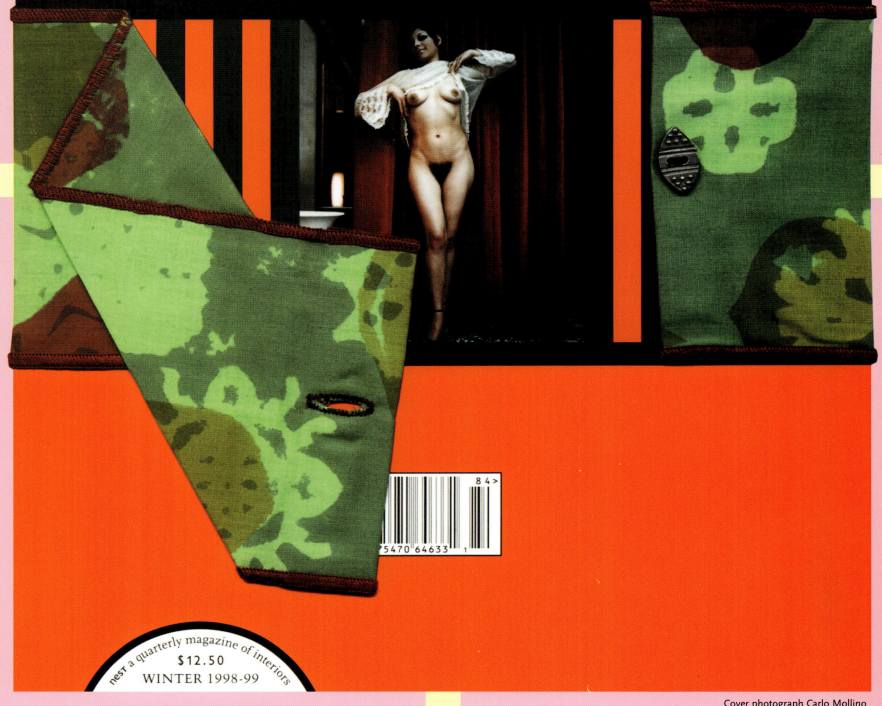

nest a quarterly magazine of interiors
$12.50
WINTER 1998-99

Cover photograph Carlo Mollino

The Worgelt Library, designed for a Park Avenue apartment, enjoys a sedate afterlife in the Brooklyn Museum. When **nest** proposed covering its chairs momentarily in Todd Oldham's fabric and bringing in a few seasonal sprigs, the museum conservator was delighted to play along, but kept close watch to make sure we did not so much as stick a pin in her "real" upholstery. In fact, Oldham and his assistants needed only scissors to get the job done.

Photograph Adam Bartos

MULELAND

Photographs Jim Goldberg with Ethan Kaplan **Original text** Kevin Killian

39

Above and following two pages: A handful of shots from our "Muleland" feature, out of a total of 39. About the two men who live and work together here Kevin Killian wrote: "The pair makes me think of the somber-eyed and dependable beasts that guide Clint Eastwood and Shirley MacLaine to border safety in *Two Mules for Sister Sara*. They're not pretentious; they do their work quietly, coolly, with a minimum of fuss and bother. You might sit and talk with them for half an hour before the glamor of their surroundings dawns on you like a slow kick in the head."

41

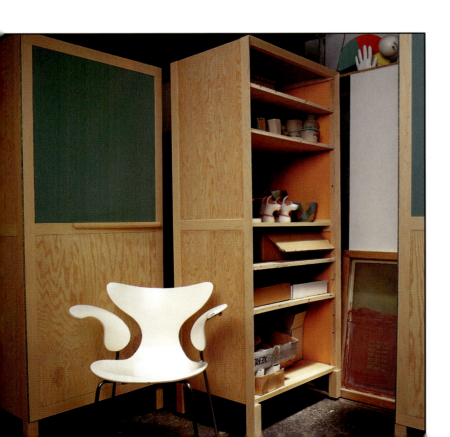

MIDNIGHT LACE

PHOTOGRAPHS
Adam Bartos

ORIGINAL TEXT
Lisa Zeiger

Above: A few of the snapshots of young prostitutes who would assume calculated poses for designer Carlo Mollino in the Turin apartment where he spent the final 14 years of his life. The marble console on which they lie scattered was made by Mollino; its sinuous, irregular outline brings to mind the rococo window frames of an earlier Turin. *Opposite page:* In his photographs for **nest**, Adam Bartos caught exactly the Mollino blend of severity and seductive surface. Pursuing psychodynamic echoes, writer Lisa Zeiger found Mollino's lair "a taut mesh of light and dark, function and fetish, secrecy and exposure." *Following page left:* Here again is the cover nude, in situ. **nest** wished to point out a formal kinship between the angular presentation of Mollino's female subjects and his furniture designs, in this case a little-known three-legged chair from the 1930s. *Following page right:* Inside Mollino's bedchamber, trompe l'oeil paper butterflies were mounted as wall décor. These, too, reminded us of just how his women were captured on film (look at the splayed brunette to the left of this caption).

Dear subscribers and others:

I'm planning a protest, but at the moment you're in for nothing more than a scolding.

The topic is ceilings. Just look up, a little above your head. Or better, lie back in bed, get comfortable, and gaze up. What do you see? A convoy of canned lights? Here a vent, there a duct, everywhere a textured waste? Oh, please God, not your own reflection!

In all probability, reader, those upper regions are a bleak pretend-neutral place left to utilities, to the Kabuki handlers of your colorful floor-tethered existence. OK, gravity we must live with, but why spend one's days in a stage set with a strip of wall, a band of decoration rising from the floor, and then a no-man's-land above? It seems deplorable to me.

Are we decorators or are we ostriches? Face up to the Other Surface, I say, and don't act like it isn't there.

Would you like to be given a birthday gift nicely wrapped on five sides, with the top left exposed, for easier opening? Convenience is not always worth the price we pay for it. And I don't think you've done your decorating job unless you've meditated about what's going on just above your head.

Like to join that protest? Stop the lunacy now!

Joseph Holtzman

Photograph Todd Oldham

PHOTOGRAPHS **Richard Barnes**   ORIGINAL TEXT **Matthew Stadler**

HOME ALONE

"This division between what is inside (knowable, graspable) and outside (foreign and strange) is the singular point on which madness pivots," concluded Matthew Stadler in his meditations on Ted Kaczynski as a murdering recluse. Kaczynski's cabin was being kept in a warehouse for its evidence of his activities and state of mind when Richard Barnes took the award-winning photograph we chose as our sole image for the Unabomber feature; here are two others from the series.

Opposite page: Christmas décor occupies the Madison Avenue store window next to the one-person homeless shelter designed by Raymond Voogt. Writer Eileen Myles spent a week's worth of nights inside the box (while a **nest**-hired security guard stood nearby) to report how it feels to a non-homeless person to do precisely that. Living in a box on a New York City sidewalk is legal, among other things,

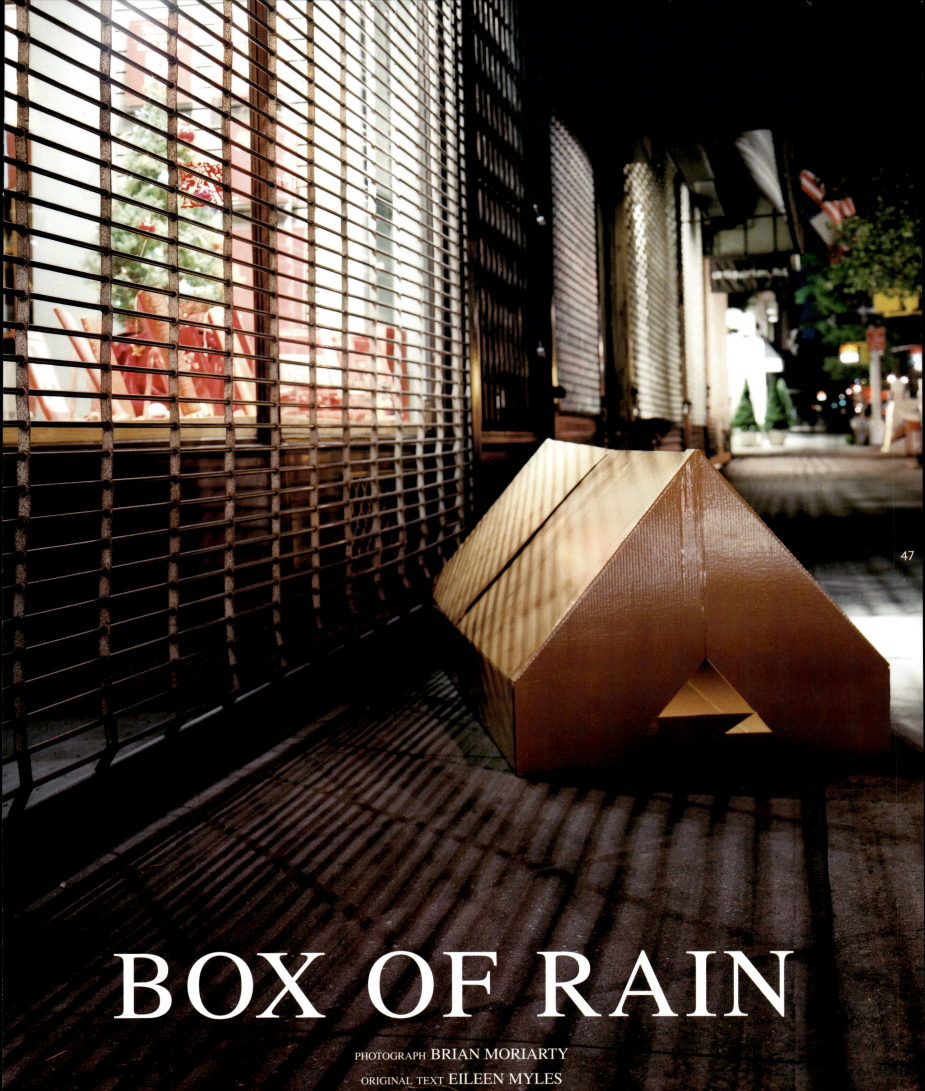

BOX OF RAIN

PHOTOGRAPH BRIAN MORIARTY

ORIGINAL TEXT EILEEN MYLES

MOSTLY MAD INDEED

Our cover story for spring 1999, "Virginia Cathouse," was the real thing, a searing investigative report on the neighborly persecution of a 46-year-old U.S. Navy program analyst for harboring upwards of one hundred and seventy cats in her Annandale, Virginia, home. The cover showed a deceptively plain bedroom scene mostly in moody blue with the odd feline curled here and there, considerably brightened by seven orange "glitter boxes" ranged about the bed. Naturally, the glitter was real and will come off if you insist.

But the true story, whoever might be to blame, stayed a sad one. When we got wind of it, the resident cat population had been reduced from 171 to 120 by local officials. Our writer, Lisa Zeiger, suspected foul play on the part of the Humane Society of Fairfax County, who in just 10 days euthanized all 51 animals they managed to get their claws on, claiming some or all to be carriers of a serious disease. And what could be the real motive for community interest in the teeming cat hostel? Zeiger began her piece by observing that "in the Middle Ages, and in colonial Salem, cats were persecuted along with their mistresses as witches' servants—conveniently silent, mysterious beings on whom to project fear of the feminine." **nest** found her take plausible. For solitary women *are* still suspect, and the more pets they take in, the more "single" they become in society's eyes. (Meanwhile the subtext of this feature was—what else?—cats as decoration.)

"Through a Glass Darkly" presented sneak photos of New Yorkers inside their apartments, captured at night from across the street. We had it on good authority that our quarry were guilty of routine exhibitionism, and they were certainly guilty of leaving their blinds up and lights on. As for us: The world, it is said, divides nicely into a half that looks in someone else's medicine cabinet and a half that doesn't. In that case, **nest** belongs to the big half.

A different voyeurism, this time all within the home, was implicit in the New York townhouse Paul Rudolph designed for himself in the 1970s. "The Tower and the Sea" (the latter being applied with poetic license to the East River) used vistas and close-up shots to reveal the aging architect's domestic masterwork and a sleek and perhaps treacherous bathhouse atmosphere in which one false step might be your last. This story contributed to a renewed interest in the Rudolph house and would help, indirectly, to secure its future.

"Lucy Ricardo: Decorator" spelled out the meaning of the comedian's evolving living room, with freeze-frames downloaded from her classic fifties television show. We followed Lucy's decorating peregrinations from set to set. An ominous shift from mildly modern to Early American took place when—along with so many others in those deeply misguided times— she forsook New York for the burbs. **nest**, by the way, believes that everyone's a decorator, though not always for the better.

Some of the most visually haunting pages in **nest**'s brief history came with "Southern Gothic" and photographer Diane Cook's award-winning images (originally produced by **nest** in duotone). They tease the soul out of a bizarrely monumental coral-rock garden in Homestead, Florida, the life work of a lonely Latvian immigrant who was missing his girl, Agnes, and perhaps more.

nest A QUARTERLY OF INTERIORS

49

0 74820 64633 5
91>

PHOTOGRAPH   MITCH EPSTEIN
ORIGINAL TEXT   SUSAN BELL

Through a Glass Darkly

These people were the only exhibitionists who were really on the job. The **nest** idea was that since other shelter magazines thrive on unacknowledged voyeurism/exhibitionism (it takes two to tango), we would bring this essentially wholesome and life-affirming phenomenon out into the open.

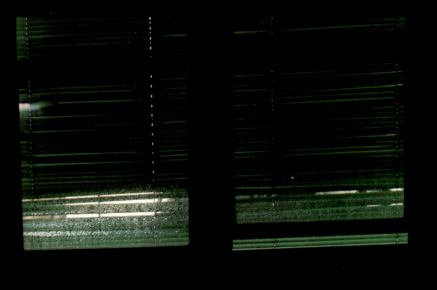

the tower and the sea

original text frederic tuten   photographs todd oldham and derry moore   todd is in the details, moore is more

The East River exposure of the Rudolph House on Beekman Place, with its cubist-inspired double-story living room and flanking mezzanines. "After clothing, house is the third skin few are able to create for themselves," Frederic Tuten wrote. Without having met Rudolph, our writer could still picture him and his male entourage: "He's a dry man on the bridge of his destroyer, circa 1950; his crew follows him and believes in him; his berth may be larger but it is as shipshape and Spartan as theirs." A Rudolph-designed chair of Lucite on castors typifies the architect's taste for hard, bare surfaces.

54

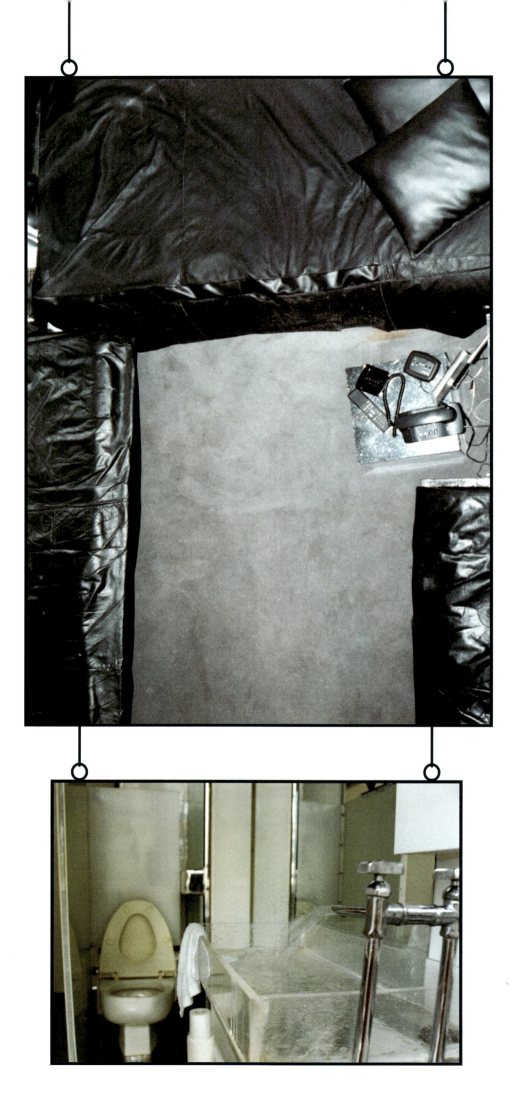

This house encouraged one to look up, down, and around corners. Tight spiral stairs, catwalks, see-through and reflecting surfaces were all installed here to incite prowlers, our photographer included, into making rounds. *Above and left:* Peering down from a catwalk into a den-bedroom clad mostly in leather, and into a bathroom with Plexiglas sink and open toilet stall. *Opposite page:* A twist of risky free-floating steel steps, their color mimicked in the gray raw silk on the walls, leading to the upper living room levels.

LUCY RICARDO: DECORATOR

photographs JASON SCHMIDT
illustrations WOUTER DOLK
original text FRANCES McCUE

Left to right, our televisions charted Ricardo's ascent to modernism and its austerities as she changed addresses in New York, and then an abrupt descent to the folksy with her remove to Connecticut. A Dutch artist, Wouter Dolk, drew these vintage television cabinets for **neѕт** after checking out catalogues of near-antiques. The issue contains many examples of his work, in particular depictions of rabbits (i.e., the Easter Bunny) in all of life's vicissitudes.

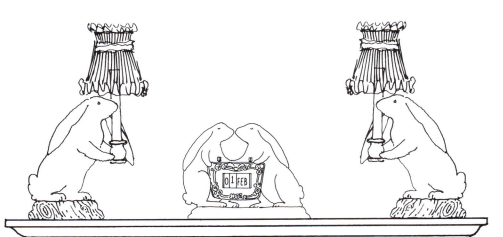

Left, **Ricardo Regency:** Ensconced in a Manhattan apartment, Lucy's first décor was department-store "traditional," with a standard trio of chintz-covered sofa, carved cabriole-legged coffee table, and fauteuil. Above the upright piano, multiple small-framed oval ornaments surround an elaborately gilt-framed oil. Behind Lucy and Ethel, baseboard, dado, and arched door moldings are emphasized by subtle paint contrasts. Two ashtrays.

Below, **Ricardo *renovato*:** Same digs, new décor, slouching toward middlebrow modern. The painted, fashionably exposed brick wall sports pictures hung at a daring diagonal; other artwork has been edited to three paintings (center). The new boxy sofa and chair, smartly tailored in wool fabric, are punctuated by single high lines of tufting. Lucy still cannot resist the Louies, with a new cabriole-legged table recalling her ancien régime. The silk-shaded brass lamp (far right) will survive all but the final upheaval. Ashtray, cigarette box, and smoking stand.

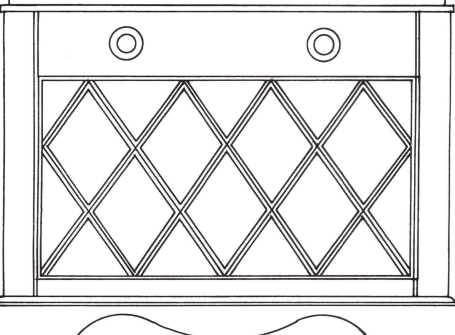

Connecticut Conquistadora: New Canaan WASP meets L.A. ranch, the sofa suspiciously similar to the dowdy chintz number in apartment number one, now garnished with a dust ruffle. The mantelpiece sports a pewter plate, Paul Revere tankards, and other mini-votives to and of the Founding Fathers. At far left, a "Colonial" rocker, probably from Ethan Allen and, at far right, a glimpse of round rag rug and Dutch doors hung with tied-back sheers. No lamps; four ashtrays.

Lucy *adornista*: In her new New York pad, Lucy goes as "contemporary" as TV will allow, installing up-to-the-minute modulars with chic, acutely pitched seats, vestigial arms, and shallow buttonless tufting in the manner of Ed Wormley. Door moldings are squared, not arched, as in the old apartment; wall decorations all but absent. The deep window embrasure behind the piano is framed by pleated pelmet and drapes, which can be drawn over the criss-crossed organdy under-curtains. Two ashtrays.

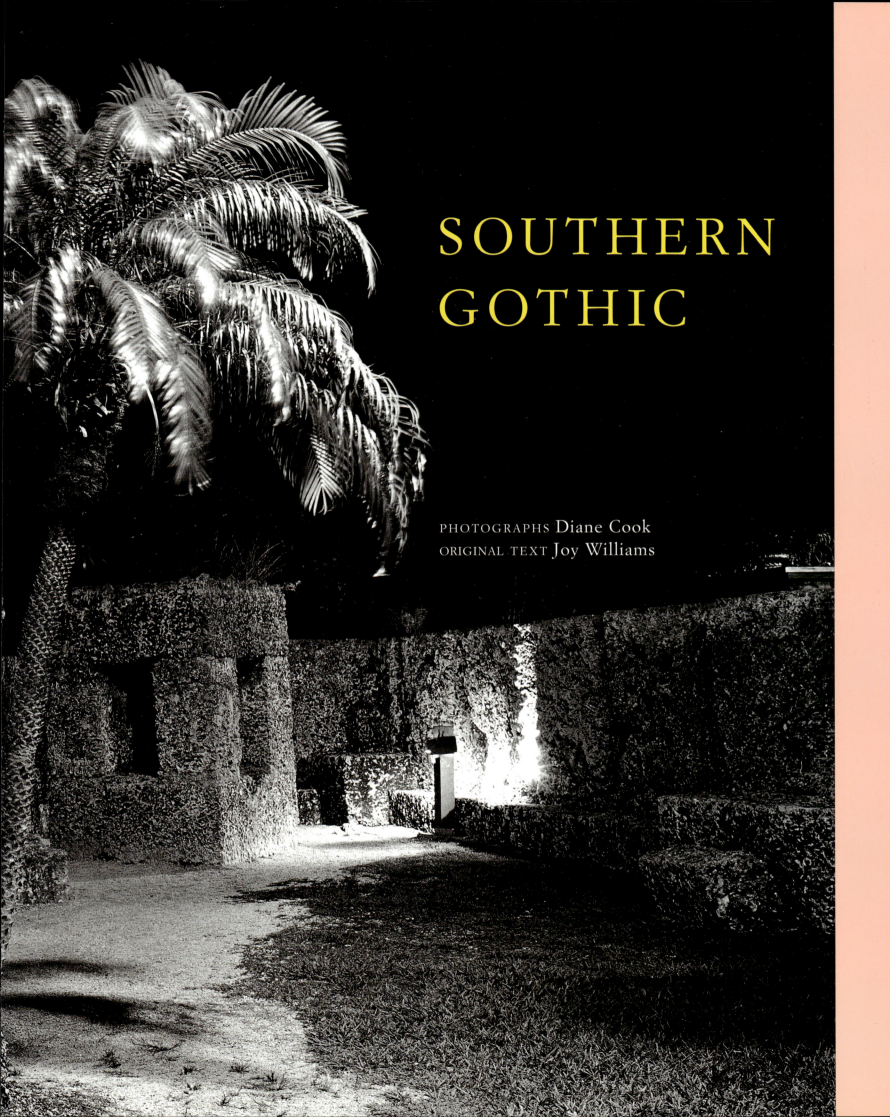

SOUTHERN
GOTHIC

PHOTOGRAPHS Diane Cook
ORIGINAL TEXT Joy Williams

Previous two pages: A sweeping view of what Ed Leedskalin built by hand over a period of 20 years, a place expressive of his own peculiar cosmology. "Ed himself may have come from the moon, or somewhere farther," our writer, Joy Williams, surmised. "When he talked about 'Sweet Sixteen,' which he did a lot, everyone presumed he was talking about that poor Agnes Scuffs of Latvia, but in fact he was not—'Sweet Sixteen' was a spaceship Ed thought might find the Coral Castle and take him home, back home to the Big Rock somewhere in space."

This page: Ed carved some of his sculptural elements after heavenly bodies. To the left is Saturn, 18 feet high and weighing as many tons; the Crescent Moon is 20 feet high and weighs 23 tons. He moved such objects without anyone's help. *Opposite page:* A 9-ton gate set in the neatly finished wall surrounding Coral Castle is so precisely balanced that a poke of the finger causes it to swing open or shut.

MOTHER KNOWS BEST

nest has never thought of itself as "like" some other magazine. Yet advertisers always ask us who are our "comparables," our direct competition. On the summer 1999 cover we staged a rude encounter between two publications that are occasionally mentioned in the same breath with **nest**. This mischief recalled those distant days of heedless play with the chemistry set, when anything might happen, and did.

"Swatch Watch: Wolf at the Door," the story that went with the cover, was one in a series of **nest** features recording the tribulations of a certain Arlene "Mother" Swatch, uptown decorator in a largely downtown world (she's the one on the left). Those who wish to may read the contributor bios that have accompanied her **nest** appearances (officially Mother is our Resident Practicing Consultant). On this occasion one learned that her formation was achieved exclusively at Montreal's Les Dames du Sacre Coeur (semicloistered at the time) and that wines of the Loire Valley are implicated in her successful Park Avenue/Palm Beach practice.

"The Squeeze Machine" took Matthew Stadler to Sitka, Alaska, where he spent the afternoon with an 11-year-old autistic boy and became acquainted with his ingenious ways of coping with an overly stimulating world. To develop this feature, **nest** appealed to the manufacturer of the "squeeze machine," a device that applies controlled pressure to the body of an autistic person in order to ease anxiety. (The manufacturer agreed to send letters to its customers in the hope of finding one who would volunteer to be our subject.)

For "Philip Johnson Redressed" no cooperation was forthcoming. We faced that most exciting of all journalistic prospects—camera non grata. So, in lieu of paying an official call at the Robert Leonhardt House on Long Island, **nest** resorted to stealth. It was well worth a few twinges of conscience (were there any?) to be able to tell the before-and-after story of hair-raising alterations inflicted on one of Johnson's classic modern houses.

In this issue, too, we published "A Philosophy of Clean," a short account by the philosopher D.L. Pughe in which Pughe's work as a housecleaner delivers her to knowledge making continued service in a particular household impossible. It is printed here in full.

Opposite page: Issue 5 rose to the challenge of a wavy die-cut. Every editorial page was laid out with these curves in mind, as one more variation on a theme. Previously we had designed around a rounded corner (issues 1 and 2) and in succeeding issues we would find other ways to up the design ante. We even hoped that advertisers, once informed of specifications for an upcoming issue, would become interested in playing our game, and some did.

Cover photograph Jason Schmidt

Swatch Watch: Wolf at the Door

photographs Jason Schmidt
original text Arlene "Mother" Swatch
Miss Swatch's gowns Albert Nipon

64

Our story line: Mother Swatch, on special assignment for **nest**, is transported to a remote, sixth-floor walkup ("tene-
ment" is her word) to inspect the work of maestro Vicente Wolf on behalf of a young bachelor, unknown to Mother and
perhaps not even socially registered. Her apprehensions will be more than justified, but Mother is a professional and
sees things through to the bitter end.

a PHILOSOPHY *of* CLEAN*

D. L. Pughe

Madame B. lived in a cliff-side home on a mountain in a tropical city where I once worked for a year. She was a round, pleasant-looking woman reminiscent of an aging stage beauty. Madame B. was from an old aristocratic family, an expert on the avant-garde theater, and she had gathered all the expatriate poets, writers, and painters round her in a salon renowned in the Islands.

Her husband was from Rumania, one of the original expressionist poets who was active in Zurich. He was small, with tiny feet and hands, and walleyed. Behind his thick goggle glasses, his right eye looked out in a direction different from the left.

I began to clean their home in winter, during the time of the monsoon rains. It was a long, winding tram ride to the top of their peak. The tram creaked and grunted around the narrow streets and always threatened to topple over the edge. When I finally entered their home, I was struck by the odd conglomeration of order and disorder filling each room. Some areas were elaborately arranged with art, like altars; others were a jumble of clutter swept into a pile, waiting uncomfortably to be

dealt with. The B.'s had few rugs and there was a mountain coolness which rose up from their tile floors which still clings to my knees.

I remember cleaning for Madame B. always on my knees, over the acres of floor in each descending level of their home. She would offer me a piece of fruit or a drink at first, but before I had made my selection she would have noticed a stain or tuft of dust which needed immediate attention. She would cry out, snap her fingers, and point at a far place on the floor. I would fill my bucket and begin to crawl towards it. Madame B. accompanied me on these sojourns, walking above me, telling me a little of her work on a famous playwright, extolling the virtues of an artist who had done a magnificent white marble bust of her when she was younger, or speaking of her health. Her "condition" gradually came to occupy most of her time and conversation. Her doctor was forcing her to diet and emphasized the seriousness with which she should approach her recovery. She worried aloud, pulled at her hair as she spoke to me, acknowledging the doctor as a

67

* Excerpted from an unpublished work.

torturer, her diet as a dismal jail. The name of her illness was never disclosed.

She would wander after me on the main floor upstairs; her husband usually sat reading in a nearby room, almost always arranged in our line of sight through an open doorway. His small hands held his book motionless before his face, his eyes moved separately, yet his ears I felt were the most active; I always knew he was listening to our conversation. And he was always wearing a hat.

I offered a little information about myself. They knew I was interested somehow in poetry and philosophy. But it was imperative to them that they know very little. I was a servant; they were from the old country. I came to understand that all their questions to me were polite but rhetorical. I might begin a reply and Madame B. would suddenly step forward, point, snap her fingers, clap her hands in the direction of a distant corner. Even though she knew I would eventually work my way there, she expressed an urgency that could not be ignored. I would crawl quickly forward, a rush toward the enemy offending her eyes, and attack it with appropriate gusto. In this way we avoided knowing each other too well through words.

But I grew to know her so well in other ways, ways that sifted through my skin and made me reel with too much knowledge when I left their house each week. In the lower level carved into the rock of the mountain, she and her husband had their bedrooms, each joined by a central room filled with primitive sculptures of all shapes and sizes. Madame B.'s bedroom had a pink tile floor; her bathroom was pink; her large bedspread and curtains were pink satin. On the wall were black-and-white photos taken in Paris, when she was young, blonde, beautiful, and apparently the only woman among a circle of handsome men at the university. She smiled out from clusters of these men, some quite young, some old and distinguished. Her light dress, the scarf around her neck, and the radiance of her smile told me how happy she was then.

A bit like the famous stage actress, the times when she was younger.

Madame B.'s bathroom was filled with blue glass bottles imported from all over the world, a veritable alchemy shop for distilling beauty from age and despair. There were creams and powders, lotions and special waters in bottles with mysterious names. All were blue. Once I accidentally knocked one over and a dark iodine-like liquid splattered all over the pink floor and into the shower made of bright pink tile which sometimes blinded me as I cleaned it. Madame B. was kind about my clumsiness, I remember, but I knew it must be hard to replace these rare liquids. And the powders she used seemed otherworldly; she evidently patted them on in thick layers for, when I went to clean her pink shower each week, there was white mud covering its floor. She gave me a child's small metal shovel and sand bucket to clear away her powdery mud.

Mr. B.'s bedroom was not at all pink, and had a distinct flavor of Uruguay, where he had once lived for a few years. Pegs along the upper perimeter of his walls each held one hat. Below, on the floor, his small shoes were arranged in a row around the floor-board, each pair underneath a hat above. The room appeared to be a place for constant changes of mood, of appearance. His desk sat at the window overlooking the turquoise bay. On his old typewriter I could see a new poem each week peeking from the carriage, always in a foreign language: Portuguese, Rumanian, French. He spoke many languages, perhaps as many as he had hats. His small single bed was covered in a bright blanket of stripes handwoven in the mountains of South America.

The room in between their bedrooms was a cacophony of sculptures, mostly small, earth-tone clay, nearly impossible to dust and clean. It was here I spent most of my time, rubbing the curves of small ceramic musicians, wiping the crowns of exotic deities, and it is where Mr. B. often passed through and disappeared into his bedroom. I would hear a bit of typing, long periods of silence, then he would drift in again, now wearing a different hat. One eye would travel over me as he passed through, the other guiding him somewhere else.

Each week when I rolled away Madame B.'s large pink satin bed to mop her floor, I found dozens of brown fluted chocolate wrappers. She must have known I would find them and sweep them away, but it was then I realized the key to intellectual life: it does not often connect to your real life. You are able to discuss an abstract persona of yourself, constructed from all that you read, know, and want to believe. But your actions may be telling you and the world something else and you are not expected to listen to them. This gap between theory and reality came to disturb me. I began to examine my own life for cloaked contradictions, and found ample evidence of the same pattern of separation within myself.

On the day I decided to quit, I felt I had grown too close to them, this odd and talented couple. I was fond of them in a way, even though I was treated more like a servant than in any other home. But Madame B.'s complaints about her diet, her worries about her health, were escalating and becoming frantic and prolonged. Her doctor was changing from a torturer into a demonic god who was trying to seal her fate. She railed against him. And this seemed to rise in proportion to the number of chocolate wrappers I found each week, the silent evidence of something she herself could not see or hear. Perhaps alone in her bedroom she became again the glamorous woman of the university where reality could not touch her. She could refuse its uncomfortable glare in this pink sanctuary.

Mr. B. came through several times on my last day, intently watching me. Madame B. had left for the grocery to purchase fresh vituperative healthy foods the doctor was forcing on her. Mr. B. was passing through in various hats. His walleye was beginning to caress my legs as I crawled around

scrubbing the floor. When he was headed toward me, his focusable eye was beginning to look directly into mine in a way that made me shudder. And he suddenly appeared, after an hour of steady typing, wearing seven hats stacked one on top of the other.

I retreated to clean Madame B.'s bathroom where it was safe to close the door. I pulled back the shower curtain and began to scoop out the grayish white mud. I found a cluster of pale mushrooms growing there, healthy and glowing pink in the odd light of this chamber. For some reason this struck me as terribly sad. An aching, sobbing feeling came over me and I realized I had come too close to their lives. I could barely tell her, when she returned that day, that I could not come anymore. I sputtered something about my other obligations. She was angry but tried to understand. Though I had not ever dreamed it was open to me at all, I knew her salon would be forever closed to me, no matter what I might do. I knew that if I met them on the street they would not notice me or recognize me out of this context of their lives. It did not make me sad but I wondered later if I would always have a hesitation about knowing intellectuals I admire too closely.

It is not that I could only accept the dirt of people I love, and not of those whose ideas I love. That has never been the case. I do not hope the thinkers I admire are clean, but simply that they recall what they consign to that dark space under their beds, an outpost of consciousness where my mop and mind travel.

I learned, after I had moved far far away, that Madame B. had died. In a large bookstore in a distant city, I found a slim volume of poems written to her by her husband. His haunted love emerged as an ethereal lament; he appeared to love her as one has always dreamed of being loved, with fierce respect and constant intensity. I felt again the cold floor in my knees, the curves of the statues, a shovel full of powder in my hands.

The graceful bolts and elegant knockers illustrated here are from a French firm's catalog published around 1905. The book's plates display fine door hardware available in a multitude of finishes and every conceivable style, from Gothic to Renaissance to Louis XVI, and for the more daring, Art Nouveau.

Philip
Johnson
Redressed

digital imaging Nick Buccalo
photograph Ezra Stoller © Esto
original text Shawn Brennan

the squeeze machine

photographs Arthur S. Aubry
original text Matthew Stadler

nest editor-in-chief Joseph Holtzman was ready to do anything to bag "Philip Johnson Redressed." Even a helicopter flyover was weighed. Eventually, poor quality photographs from a land-based photographer were procured and from these images, which would have been illegal to publish, **nest** synthesized a perfectly legal computer image documenting the changes present-day owners have wrought upon Johnson's Robert Leonhardt House (built in 1956). To facilitate comparison, our simulated color image was printed on a transparent acetate sheet and laid over another image (black and white) of the structure in its pristine state. **nest** was charitable in describing how the two contrasting wings of blank brick and cantilevered glass of Johnson's flat-roofed house had been unified with a veneer of Tudor half-timbering, iron railings, and ornamental peaked roofs. "The picturesque effect," we opined, "shows that when you start with a great design, you need only to fill in the details to finish it off." (There is indeed something fascinating about the fate of Modernism.)

Many **nest** stories have extended the concept of the "room," among them "The Squeeze Machine." Being closely held by the machine offered young Matthew the sense of security most people gain from being enclosed within the usual four walls. *Above:* The squeeze machine at work, with Matthew inside. This contraption was invented by Temple Grandin, an autistic woman who first encountered a similar calming device for cattle and, trying it on herself, discovered that the evenly applied pressure had a deeply calming effect. The commercial product for humans, in comfortable padded vinyl, is made by the Therafin Corporation of Mokena, Illinois.

POODLES AND OTHERS

A holier-than-thou attitude may be foreign to **nest**, but with this issue (fall 1999) we succumbed, the body of the magazine being perforated clear through in four places. The holes, nearly a quarter inch in diameter and marked here in hot pink, fell along a rectangular grid whose mathematics (odd) could be reckoned from the feature "Ideal Lodging," where the pattern became explicit. Our texts and graphics ignored them at their peril. Naturally, we played with the possibilities (as on the cover, with its line of decoys), and so did some of our advertisers, who were tipped off in advance.

The lower left-hand hole went right through Guido, a poodle whose guardians are none other than Joseph Holtzman and Carl Skoggard, the author of this sentence. Why, you might ask, would they allow such a thing? And what about his tumorlike attire? Guido wore it for a summer, proudly enough we thought, in honor of designer Rei Kawakubo's somewhat similar line for humans. Still, there were people who saw only red when Guido chanced by. Our editor-in-chief dealt with the evidently galling "hump cut" in his letter to readers (reprinted). Controversy aside, it is worth noting how **nest** seems to find exotic material so close to home.

From time to time we go to great trouble to provide readers with toys in the form of inserts. "Goya's Quinta del Sordo: Reconstructed" included a four-page gatefold on heavy stock; on it were printed the elements needed to build a 3-D model of the artist's long vanished country house. The adventurous reader could detach these perforated elements and proceed, consulting mother wit. A correctly assembled model disclosed Goya's Black Paintings in their original setting and arrangement on the interior walls, thanks to detective work done by **nest** decorative arts editor Shawn Brennan.

"Stalking Montmartre's Blue Angel" called for detective work because our subject balked in midstream. Michou, owner of the most durable drag cabaret in Paris, did grant **nest**'s writer an interview and consented to the usual preliminary snapshots, but when our photographer sought to arrange a photo shoot, the Capricious One blew him off without so much as "poof to you." We came through with a mix of the writer's snaps of Michou's impressively banal apartment and external surveillance shots taken in a spirit of revenge.

Another Parisian, Henri Samuel, was further proof of something **nest** finds fascinating: the unexpected domestic choices made by creative men and women. Samuel, high priest of ancien régime décor who, in Mitchell Owens's words, regenerated "the splendors of the past for the monarchs of café society," made the grand salon of his last home a daring mélange of neon and Empire chimneypieces, Directoire and disco. Who knows what you'll discover when you visit an artist?

Cover photograph ANTOINE BOOTZ
nest logo photograph NINA KATCHADOURIAN

nest A QUARTERLY OF INTERIORS

FALL 1999 • $10.00

74820 64633

93>

If British justices wanted to get even more laughs, they would don poodle wigs as did the contributors to issue 6. **nest** editor-in-chief Joseph Holtzman wore the whole thing, live, for his letter-page photo.

Dearest Reader:

Some people don't like my Guido—the way he looks, that is. Just last night a woman passed us and said, under her breath, "Mean thing to do to your poodle." She was referring to his new "hump cut," which I thought up as homage to fashion designer Rei Kawakubo (in this issue Guido's going to give you an expert scratch-and-sniff tour of her recently opened Chelsea store).

I, of course, love the cut—and I love my dog and would never do anything mean to him. Guido, a show-circuit retiree when we met, is not ashamed to get dressed up or get shorn and takes his decoration as it comes. He's as content with the current lumpy look as he was with his previous overall-shaggy, boy-next-door cut. His dignity is not a hair affair.

Hair, however, is a supersensitive issue for *us*, one of those "contested sites" everyone's so hot about. Strange how poodle hair is drawn into the all-too-human vortex of class and gender. Guido's boyish overall cut (which he kept for three years) encouraged quite a few we met in Central Park to confide their disdain for the usual effeminate poodle frippery. Now these new humps of his are driving another subset of our species crazy.

Come into the **nest** examining room and let Dr. Holtzman diagnose your condition. Hmm. . . If you think Guido's dignity is being injured by this homage to Kawakubo, I'd say you're projecting. It's really *my* aesthetic that's bothering *you*. But why let every challenge to convention become a personal insult? (That's paranoid).

74

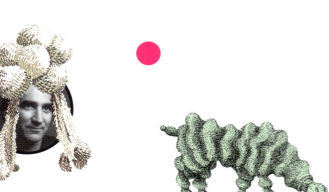

Joseph Holtzman

Poodles and poodle wigs **Wouter Dolk**

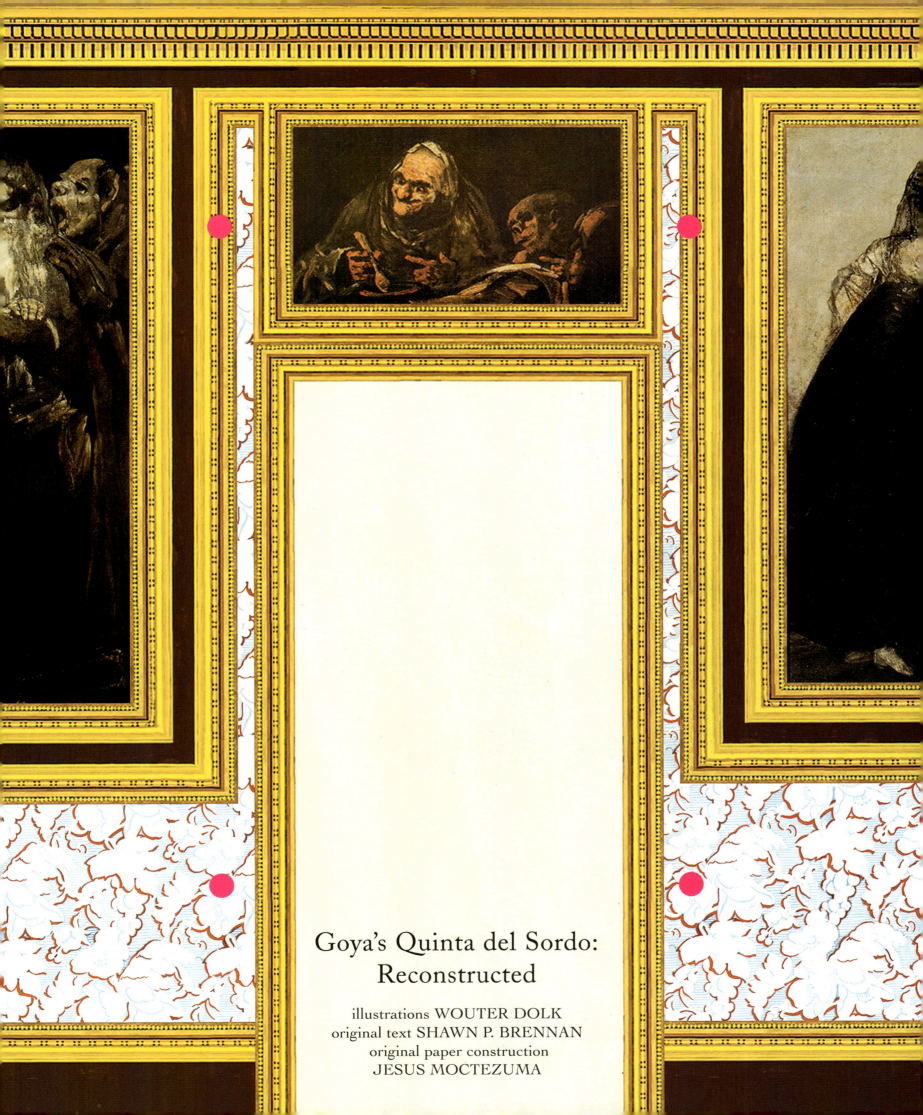

Goya's Quinta del Sordo: Reconstructed

illustrations WOUTER DOLK
original text SHAWN P. BRENNAN
original paper construction
JESUS MOCTEZUMA

Paying equal attention to paintings and décor, **nest** decorative arts editor Shawn Brennan recreated the main two rooms of Goya's country house near Madrid as these would have appeared in the 1860s, before the artist's painted-on-plaster masterpieces were stripped from the walls. Brennan examined the full set of negatives of 14 photographs taken of the paintings in situ during those same years, and thus had more information at his disposal than did a previous researcher who also attempted the reconstruction. **nest**'s interpretation of the west wall of the ground floor (with the paintings *A Final Pilgrim, The Witchy Brew,* and *Leocadia*) appears on page 75; the page opposite shows a section of the south wall of the second floor (with *The Cudgel Fight*). Because the wallpapers could not be definitively identified from the old photographs, their patterns (and colors) were adapted from contemporary examples found in scholarly publications. Our deductions about the surfaces of moldings were based on their apparent light-reflecting properties. Goya's rural retreat has long since disappeared before an expanding city.

All the elements needed for your own model of Goya's country house with its newly reconstructed interiors came on a quadruple gatefold of heavy stock paper (right). Windows were shown in black (their shape and size being deduced from fenestrations of other Spanish rural houses of the period). Several funnel pieces were included as aids for peering into the completed model. We were indebted to Jesus Moctezuma, the Italian paper-model wizard, for its design.

nest adapts: When Michou refused to let our photographer in, he must have imagined that this story was dead. Not so. We turned it into a gumshoe's dossier with KGB-style typesetting and the crude snapshots taken earlier by our writer ("...and I took the opportunity to snap a picture. Responding with an ear-to-ear Carol Channing smile, to underscore his stiff blond coiffure, he froze graciously..."), supplemented by outside surveillance images.

STALKING MONTMARTRE'S BLUE ANGEL
Snapshots and original text Bruce Benderson
Surveillance photos Luke Panisset

Eight floors above a small, gated street in Montmartre reigns nightclub entrepreneur Michou, the French Liberace, perpetually sporting a blindingly azure blazer and Jackie O.-style blue-tinted glasses. For thirty-five years, Michou's claim to fame has been his tiny club at 80 rue des Martyrs, Chez Michou, featuring decent Picard cuisine and a much-loved Montmartre drag show. In this cramped cartoon paradise whose red walls are hung with extravagantly gilded mirrors, performers reject the literal exactness of American female impersonation in favor of Molière-style caricature. Their exaggerated send-ups of Edith Piaf, Josephine Baker, Madonna, or Liza Minnelli hearken back to a time when royalty could be parodied but never directly criticized—on pain of death. Both Hollywood and European royalty, from Lauren Bacall to Mireille do the pilgrimage up the steep Montmartre hillside to the little of the minuscule stage and pay

Their exass

Minnelli hearken back to a time when royal—

criticized—on pain of death.

Both Hollywood and European royalty, from Lauren Bacall to Mireille Mathieu, have made the pilgrimage up the steep Montmartre hillside to the little club to face their images in the distorted mirror of the minuscule stage and pay homage to their beloved Michou. Little did we think that such a touted French "institution" would prove to be such an egotistical diva. But, alas, what started innocently as an attempt to celebrate Michou's extravagant apartment became a battle of wits between the willfully perverse club owner and Nest's hired paparazzo.

On a peaceful spring morning, last May, as the darling of tout Montmartre was throwing on his pressed white pants and signature blue blazer, I waited with my reporter's pad and disposable camera in his entranceway (boastfully decorated with all the gold 45s he recorded long ago). Michou's canvas-crowded foyer, into which I was next ushered, was even more lavishly decorated. "Those paintings? They are just 'Montmartrois' [paintings by neighborhood artists]," my host scoffed, as he yanked me away toward the living room. But craning my neck back, methinks I spied some genuine major and minor masters, such as Picasso, Lorjou and Gen Paul.

The "Blue Angel" of Montmartre ostentatiously installed himself on his overstuffed couch (upholstered in a flower pattern of blue and white to match his

7:49 A.M.   TUESDAY.
SURVEILLANCE OF SUBJECT'S MONTMARTE APARTMENT BEGINS.

4:45 P.M.   WEDNESDAY.
NO SIGN OF OCCUPANCY OR MOVEMENT
IN APARTMENT.

9:36 A.M.   THURSDAY.
MICHEL CATTY, A.K.A. MICHOU, SIGHTED ON STREET.

Samuel at Ninety

photographs Christoph Kicherer *original text* Mitchell Owens

MICHOU WAS UNCOOPERATIVE, BUT SO TOO WAS HENRI SAMUEL, WHO DIED YEARS BEFORE MITCHELL OWENS ATTEMPTED TO DECODE THOSE COMPLEX SHIFTS OF TASTE IN THE DECORATOR'S FINAL APARTMENT. THE MEASURED ELEGANCE OF SAMUEL'S BEDROOM AND PERSONAL SITTING ROOM SEEMED TO REBUT EVERY TRENDY GESTURE, YET HIS GRAND SALON WITH ITS DISTINCTLY 1970S FLAVOR SUGGESTED "NIGHTS SLUMMING RÉGINE'S IN THE COMPANY OF BOYS IN BLACK LEATHER." OUR WRITER SURMISED THAT ENTERING THIS ROOM FOR THE FIRST TIME, THE CONVENTIONALLY MINDED WOULD IMAGINE THEY'D COME UPON "A DUCHESS SHOOTING CRAPS IN MONTPARNASSE." BOLD (BORDERING ON RECKLESS) MIXING OF STYLES WAS EVIDENCE THAT SAMUEL HAD FINALLY DISCOVERED HIMSELF IN THE MOST HEDONISTIC OF DECADES. *Above:* SAMUEL IN HIS APARTMENT (HE DIED IN 1996 AT THE AGE OF 93). *Following two pages:* A LONG VIEW OF THE SALON, IN WHICH RON FERRI'S SQUARE PLEXIGLAS COFFEE TABLE WITH NEON INTERIOR WAS THE CENTER OF A SEATING GROUP FOR WHICH A CHESTNUT VELVET SOFA WAS PAIRED WITH CA. 1971 PHILIPPE HIQUILY CHAIRS OF PLEXIGLAS, BRASS, AND FUR.

DARKNESS VISIBLE

A dark enigmatic room, its rear wall perhaps only midnight-blue sky, opened onto the front cover of **nest** 7 (winter 1999-2000). Even more elusive was our back cover, on which the same ineffable blue hung in unrelieved blackness without cues of perspective. Here readers were supposed to construct cheerful modular furniture using green and lavender T-shapes of stick-on vinyl that came on an insert with the feature "Vinyl Nest" (a report on modular furniture designed by Tom Dixon).

The conceit that you held a room in your hands was enhanced by a second yellow spine running down the middle of the front cover and hinting at an otherwise transparent near wall (we gleefully tacked that stepchild of design, the bar code, onto it). And since the season of giving and receiving was again upon us, one could also imagine that the yellow ribbon with our logo ran along two sides of a package. QED: **nest** was indeed handing readers a spooky little place as a holiday gift, but it was up to you to do the furnishing.

In **nest** 7, Joseph Holtzman's own kitchen appeared along with his editor's letter, which we reprint in full. Once more, promising material had been found close to home, closer in fact than ever. By now we were looking for a special "up front" feature for each issue to run against ad pages. (In keeping with the wishes of advertisers, most magazines mix ads and editorial freely throughout. Apart from its up front story, **nest** treats its editorial pages as a single block uninterrupted by ads.)

"City of the Dead" and "Splendor in the Glass," which came one after the other in **nest** 7, provided the kind of contrast that our readers crave. The first took them to an ancient graveyard in Cairo, where half a million people live in the tombs; the second showed a grand Paris apartment done up in a dizzy panoply of mock-historical French styles rich enough to choke on.

"A House Without Dolls" offered Laurie Simmons's images of the interiors of the Stettheimer dollhouse, a prize possession of the Museum of the City of New York. **nest** would not show the human figures and Christmas décor that had crept into this unique miniature over the years, and less the clutter, Carrie Stettheimer's rooms revealed their astonishing full measure of fancy and delicacy. (From now on, we hear, the museum plans to keep the exhibit pristine.)

For those who might frown on our taking Christmas out of the Stettheimer dollhouse, "Cookie Monster" had sculptor Nayland Blake lining his mother's bedroom with ten-inch gingerbread squares on the **nest** nickel. But this was not only a prodigious gift from a son to his mother; readers were given a recipe for gingerbread wallpaper, 2,708 square feet of it, along with installation hints. Photos by Nan Goldin and a text by Pulitzer Prize winner Michael Cunningham made "Cookie Monster" an all-star affair.

"Bitch Lounge" introduced a new piece by sculptor Tom Sachs (its realization was another **nest** commission). The ambiguities of his *Bitch Lounge* emerged in a 5-photo sequence of a young female subject doing her best to appear elegant while "bitch lounging" and gradually disrobing. The feature ended with one more burst of holiday charity—an announcement that Sachs's work was for sale at $11,000 per unit from "**nest** products." Soon after, when our magazine was proposed for a national award, we were nearly disqualified for having so blatantly spiced this particular feature with commerce. Yes, we assured the nominators, the ad was just a joke—and we're still laughing. We won.

Opposite page: A sparing application of stamped aluminum foil, for example on the near edge of the floor tiles, brightened up this cover. It was the AC/DC spirit of Christmas capitalism that made us blare "MAKE YOUR OWN COVER WITH OUR FREE TOY INSIDE $12.50."

n
T **e**
s

A QUARTERLY OF INTERIORS

n e s t

MAKE YOUR OWN COVER WITH OUR FREE TOY INSIDE $12.50

WINTER 1999/2000

Dearest reader,

Sound the alarum on pot and pan! Man your sculleries! The Manhattan Kitchen Wars are on.

As such affairs go, ours began innocently enough. Having just fired my last gangly, oversized Norwegian cook (who deep-fried himself right out of a job), I was aching to resurface those drab and greasy walls.

Peacock splendors of a new paint scheme were already emerging, ever so lovingly, when what do you suppose happened? Across the way, in the kitchen window of some grander establishment, a hand-scrawled sign appeared, bearing the single word **"UGLY!"** in very large letters. At first I was hurt, but then I got a little ugly myself. You know how decorators are.

Can you get over the occupants of a floor-to-ceiling mahogany-veneered kitchen with lacquered brass fittings (and antique hokum on the one wall I see clearly) telling *me* about ugly? It's the big house on the corner talking down to the little house out back. Or chaste and dignified (rudely) calling Joseph and his coat of many colors to order.

Being one who abhors any letting of blood, I took at least two minutes to meditate my revenge. And here it is: You, reader, are to decide who's got the pretty kitchen and who not. Just flip to our current feature "Kitchen Wars" and compare the two.

The only thing I ask is that you please refrain from diplomacy. If you can't say something nasty, don't write. Four-letter words are fine, of course. May the prettiest kitchen win!

Joseph Holtzman

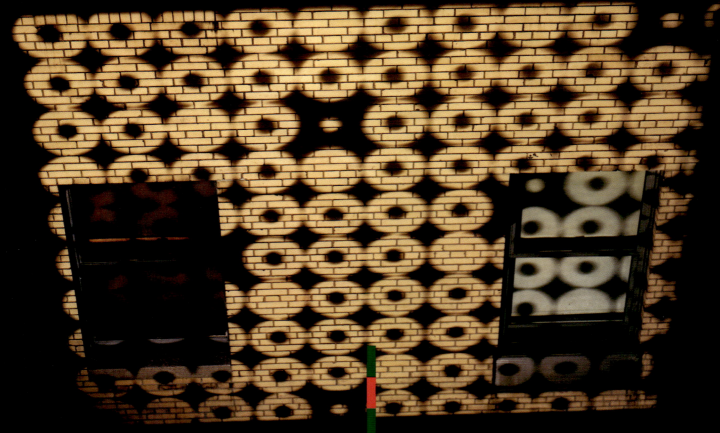

88

Photograph Jason Schmidt

CITY OF THE DEAD

PHOTOGRAPHS Richard Barnes ORIGINAL STORY Naguib Mahfouz
TRANSLATION Raymond Stock

This page and following page: Those who live in the tombs of old Cairo, which have existed for more than a thousand years and are an important monument of early Islamic architecture, enjoy unusual space and the comfort of knowing their walls are solid. Today, the five square miles of ancient cemeteries may house as many as half a million people. Inhabitants are either squatters or renters who have made arrangements with the owners of large family mausoleums. Unfortunately, Cairo's expansion is threatening the existence of the cemeteries, and at least one is soon to be "redeveloped." For this feature, **nest** commissioned the first English translation of "The Rose Garden," a 1994 story by the Nobel Prize–winning Egyptian writer Naguib Mahfouz that concerns plans to move a Cairo graveyard.

SPLENDOR
in the
GLASS

PHOTOGRAPHS
JEAN-LOUIS GARNELL

ORIGINAL TEXT
DAVID PLANTE

São Schlumberger's apartment in Paris, comprehensively decorated by Gabhan O'Keeffe, deserved full-dress treatment, and **nest** gave it 20 pages. Our notice for the room shown here: "Articulated silver animals are perched on an amboyna wood table that runs the length of the dining room. O'Keeffe designed all the furniture for this space, from the Ottoman-striped chairs to the buffet and console that hold a collection of antique silver. The sheen of the precious metal is reflected in the silk tree-of-life drapes, the carved and gilded urns, and the scrolling beaten copper frieze. The buffet's oeil-de-boeuf repeats the one above the dining room entrance from the salon, both windows being screened with a grid of glass rods and orbs. Variations on themes are played from room to room; the dominant color of this chamber was just a lively accent in the salon before."

One of the sideboards ranged along a wall of the Schlumberger dining room. *Opposite page*: A view of Madame Schlumberger's library. If our captions told one story, our writer, novelist David Plante, told another. "She invited Gabhan and me to *souper*, and while we ate a soufflé she talked peacefully about the very easy deaths of people in her and her husband Pierre's family. We were in the grand salon, where a dining table had been set up next to an enormous fish, designed by François Lalanne, the flank of which opened up to serve as a sideboard. The salon could hold a hundred people easily, but we three sat in it alone and never felt lonely. It occurred to me that, as charged as the rooms were, there was a basic sense of simple and intimate accommodation to them."

Photograph Katharina Bosse, *Untitled*, 1995, from the series "from outside/from inside"

A House Without Dolls

The Stettheimer dollhouse feature came with remarkably intimate in-and-out-of-focus images by Laurie Simmons, whose art is so often about such tiny places. Maureen Howard's text told of the celebrated Stettheimer sisters, Florine, Ettie, and Carrie, and how the last-named, less artistically forward in life, may have achieved the most lasting work with her marvelous replica of the Stettheimer family home, a leading salon for New York artists of the interwar era. Among its wonders are tiny paintings and sculptures contributed by Archipenko, Lachaise, and Duchamp. In his captions, **nest**'s decorative arts editor Shawn Brennan traced the alterations and accretions to the dollhouse since Carrie Stettheimer's death. The accretions were removed before our images were taken.

PHOTOGRAPHS LAURIE SIMMONS ORIGINAL TEXT MAUREEN HOWARD

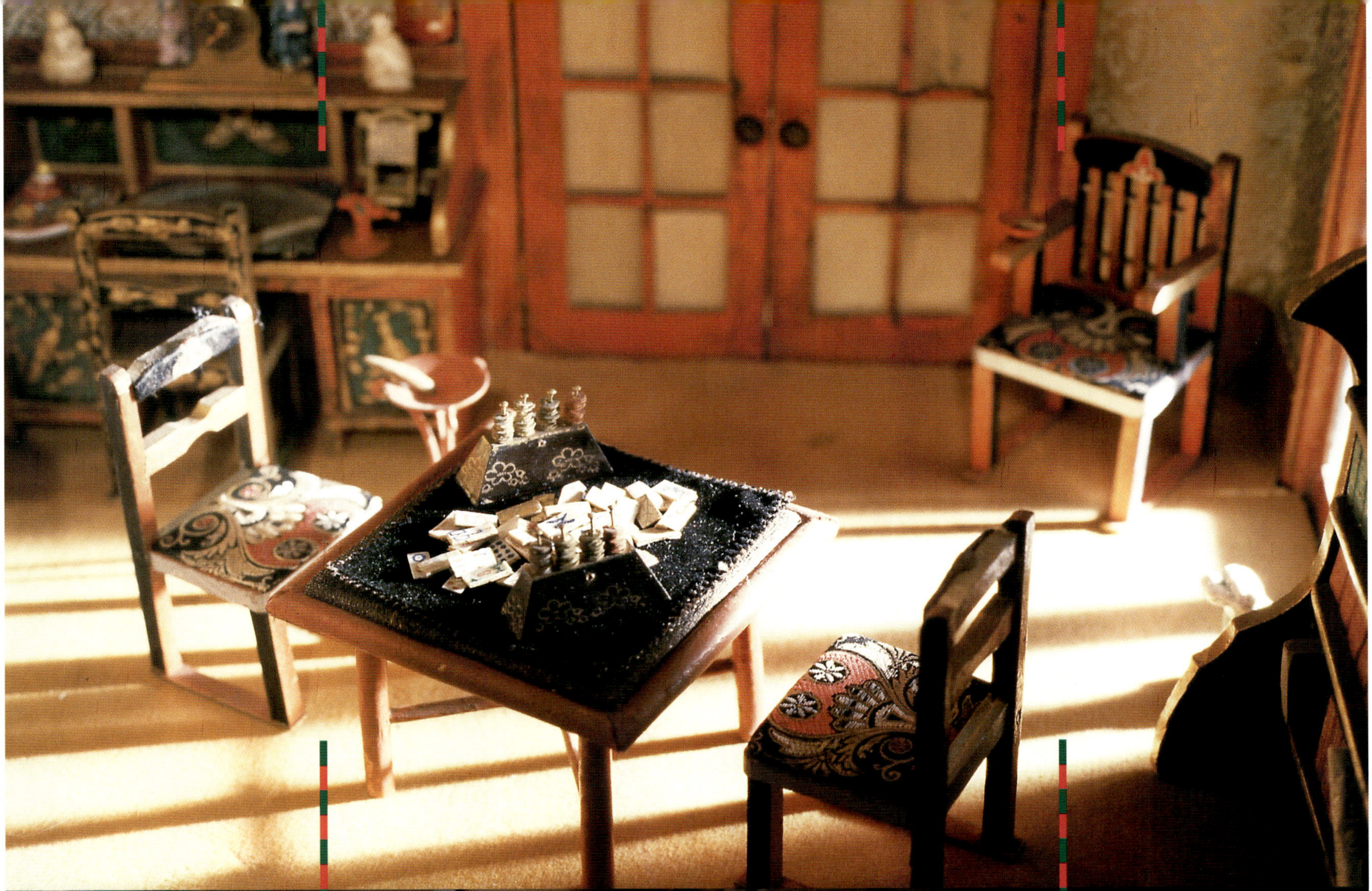

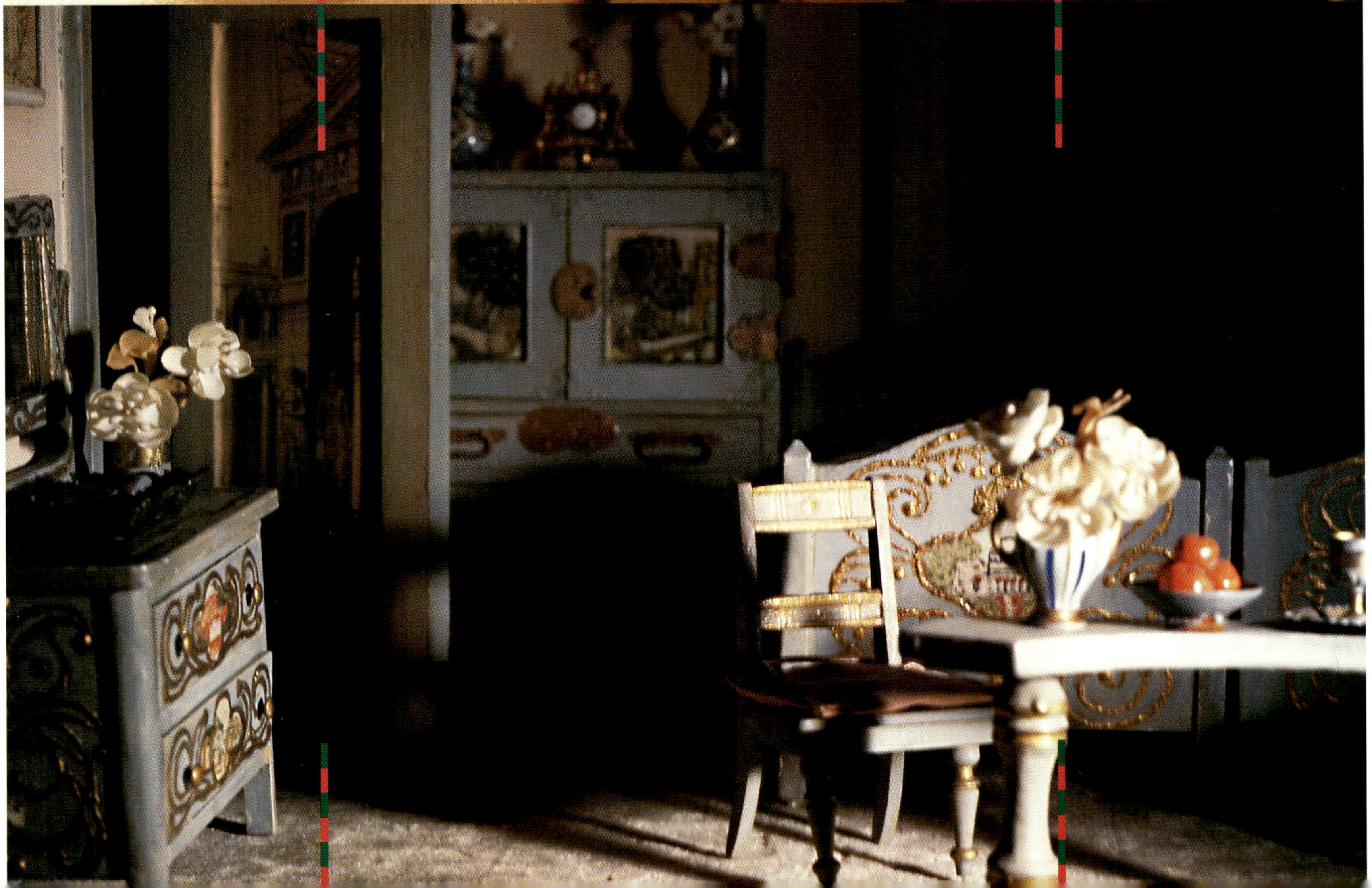

Travel East
Travel West
After all
Home's Best
1933

cookie
monster

PHOTOGRAPHS NAN GOLDIN
ORIGINAL TEXT MICHAEL CUNNINGHAM
COOKIES BAKED BY ELENI

Portrait of the artist: Nayland Blake leaning in the entryway to his mother's bedroom, which he wallpapered with 400 pounds of gingerbread at **nest**'s behest. "Pigging out for an hour or so" was her express wish after seeing Blake's installation piece *Corollary.* Feeding—nurturing a parent—was at the bottom of this bedroom installation. We hoped readers would be similarly enthusiastic when we provided them a scratch 'n sniff page as well as professional instructions, courtesy of Eleni's of New York, for baking enough gingerbread to cover a whole apartment.

GINGERBREAD WALLPAPER

Yield: about 2,708 square feet

3 cups baking soda

2 cups ground cloves

180 pounds regular flour

2 pounds ground ginger

30 pounds household molasses

2 pounds blackstrap molasses

80 pounds dark-brown sugar

33 pounds granulated white sugar

16 pounds light-brown sugar

56 pounds sweet unsalted butter

2 pounds white vinegar

280 extra-large eggs

In a separate bowl combine dry ingredients. In a mixing bowl beat butter and sugar together. Add eggs, beat well. Add vinegar, mix well. Add molasses and beat until combined. Add flour mixture and beat until combined.* Cover and chill the dough for at least 2 hours or until easy to handle.

Cut a template out of cardboard for a 10-inch by 10-inch square. Roll portions of the dough out to 1/4-inch thickness. Lay template on top of dough and, using a baking knife, cut out tile. Lay gingerbread-dough tile on lightly greased cookie sheet. Bake in a preheated 325-degree oven until crisp. Repeat 324 times.

Installation Hints: Line walls with sheet plastic to protect, and use picture-hanger nails to mount tiles to the walls. Tiles can be cut with a utility knife. Unfortunately, gingerbread wallpaper is not recommended for humid climates, so this prohibits luxurious soaks in your ginger-scented bathroom.

*Eleni recommends using a 140-quart Hobart commercial mixer.

98

ILLUSTRATION WOUTER DOLK

SCRATCH
/SNIFF
ZONE

LETTERS TO nest

The potshots and perfunctory praise filling our letter bins have been fun, but frankly they're not enough. It's hard making a magazine to a chorus of mere pleasantries (more often un-pleasantries), so **nest** *hired three discerning readers to scrutinize our first six issues and give us their critiques. We paid our hired correspondents $600 each for their letters. Here are the first three.—* **Matthew Stadler,** *Literary Editor*

SUSAN YELAVICH,
Cooper-Hewitt, National Design Museum, Smithsonian Institution

It was the stripes. I'll admit it. Amidst the eye-crossing, hysterical profusion of magazines at my local news emporium **nest** beckoned. Those handsome black and brown bands with their mysterious flocked tattoo got me. That was fall of 1998. Since then, my fledgling crush has blossomed into full-fledged lust—object lust.

Sensual and physical, **nest**—the magazine as object—transcends its status as paper ephemera, bypasses the recycling pile, and insinuates itself into the world of things kept and loved. Each issue is a "nest" to the domiciles it shelters, a nest in a permanent state of remodeling. The prospect of each season's makeover sets up a titillating mood of anticipation.

How many magazines do you have to undress to open? When winter '98-'99 came wrapped in a Todd Oldham printed fabric, secured with a bona fide button, my pretense of resistance was futile. The real seduction, of course, took place in the act of opening it. Peel away Oldham and find a woman lifting her dress for Carlo Mollino's designing eye.

Never skin deep, each transformation of **nest** tweaks our expectations, sometimes literally cutting through the pages (fall '99), or throwing us a curve (summer '99). The genius here is in understanding the touch factor: Magazines are made to be handled, as every latte bar worth its froth can attest.

The uninhibitedly sexual nature of the project is a breath of fresh air. Almost nothing is ever said about this aspect of human nature as a critical design force. Aren't our homes just an extension of our sartorial plumage, muted mating calls that advertise our fundamental selves?

Even so, the truth of the matter is that to keep my affections, the chemical attraction had to lead to an affair of the heart and the mind. **nest** offers both between the covers of its utopian world where rich and poor live side by side with neighbors who are artists, writers, curators, even philosophers (I'm thinking of D.L. Pughe's piece on Spinoza last fall).

An article on women's prison cells at the New Mexico Women's Correctional Facility is given equal time with a piece on Garouste and Bonetti's rococo rehab for a scion of Hong Kong. Ann Lauterbach's rumination on Nina Katchadourian's silken spider web repairs is the *non plus ultra* of "be it ever so humble. . . ." An essay on Ted Kaczynski's Montana cabin proves that empty houses are always haunted. No story is missing a protagonist. Dead or alive, in the flesh or in spirit, someone's always home. No stale decorating ideas here. Design is understood as an integral facet of being human.

But back to what attracted me in the first place—stripes, polka dots, checks, prints, and above all color! Working for the museum that has the largest wallpaper collection in the country, I'm bound to have a soft spot for this kind of retinal opulence. If the typography isn't up to snuff (according to my betters in this field), I can be forgiving because it's ensconced in an Alice-in-Wonderland vortex of pattern.—*Susan Yelavich*

MATTHEW SLOTOVER,
Cofounder & Editor, *frieze* magazine

"I'm against the useful in every way," Pauline de Rothschild is quoted as saying in issue 3 of **nest**. "Uselessness is rare, sometimes beautiful." De Rothschild, who died in 1976, would have liked **nest**. It's truly useless. No news or reviews, no sections, hardly anything topical—why would anyone buy it?

I bought the first couple of issues of **nest**—I like first issues; I'm a fan of some of the magazine's writers, and the design was, umm, original. I leafed through it, read a little, and pretty much forgot about it until I was asked to write this letter, and was sent the next few issues. Now obliged to actually, you know, read the magazine, I was surprised. The writing was almost uniformly excellent—clear, entertaining, and thought-provoking. In my experience of design and interiors magazines, this is rare. The magazine's mission, to reveal something about people in the way they decorate their homes, became clearer. **nest**'s style (part anthropology, part psychoanalysis, part design history) and subject matter (eclectic) are both unusual in magazines, and welcome.

I like the sociological studies, such as the photographs of bedrooms in the women's correctional facility, the piece on Matthew the autistic 11-year-old, and Lisa Zeiger's article on her own Manhattan apartment. I love the crazy individualist features, like Ed Leedskalin's coral carvings, the Jan Pol house as described by Robert Gober, and Kristin Kierig, the cat lady. But I've seen enough interiors in **nest** that are extraordinary only for the fact that they're piled with stuff their inhabitants couldn't bear to throw away. This aesthetic is as dull and clichéd as the designer minimalism that **nest** appears to be reacting against. Oh, and please lose the Fine Swaggers. It's not funny.

    nest's art director also happens to be the editor-in-chief, and presumably also the owner of the magazine. This is a pretty rare situation, and one that has led to the visual excess that you're holding now. As someone who works on a magazine, it pains me to think of the time and money that must have gone into the rounded corners, drilled holes, and samples of fabric and wallpaper. Nice try, but for me, they weren't worth it, though I must admit to enjoying watching the editorial and advertising pages work around the holes in issue 6. More generally, the art direction is too much. The typography is not good—occasionally, as in issue 2, appalling—and the design sometimes detracts enormously from the great texts and photography. Tone it down, or let someone else have a go.

    It is very unusual to find a glossy, reasonably priced magazine, as intelligent and original as **nest**, that follows no discernible PR agenda. It's also rare for a magazine to grow less and less predictable, as **nest** has. One article in issue 6—Julie Newmar's garden—took my breath away. The initial interest is a fairly camp, humorous one, but it turns by the end of the piece into something truly touching. What a scoop.—*Matthew Slotover*

REM KOOLHAAS,
Architect and founder of the firm OMA in Rotterdam,
The Netherlands

Although its editors go through extremes of reticence to avoid the appearance of ideology, **nest**, after six issues that have appeared at the end of a decade otherwise characterized by *Wallpaper* and *Martha Stewart Living*, can no longer hide its manifesto-like ambitions.

    Covering a spectrum that ranges from the seedy to the esoteric, from the effete to the eccentric, from the frankly privileged to the materially challenged, its focus on the inner life of interiors, its uncovering and dissemination of spaces that, literally, no amount of money could ever buy or construct, are at this point in our culture highly polemical. Even if it is with an almost adamant avoidance of militancy, its documentation of inimitable accumulations of customized, unique, eccentric, and personal values, inevitably has the effect of a counter-movement. At first sight eclectic and bizarre, **nest** finally is an anti-materialistic, idealistic magazine about the hyperspecific in a world that is undergoing radical leveling, an "interior design" magazine hostile to the cosmetic.

    Awkward, maudlin, academic, dry, pompous, but also striking, funny, moving, its intimate vignettes have the capacity to truly amaze us—like Mussolini's presence

in LA in the twenties—and to reveal indirectly how crude and ignorant our current narratives are.

    nest goes for the jugular of the secretive. Sometimes the intimacies revealed are almost voyeuristically painful. It is significant that in the era of celebrity and the relentless confessional, the glimpses of previously hidden lives that **nest** reveals are shocking in their acute, slightly obscene quality. They show the extent of editing, pruning, and laundering that the professional press of revelation performs before launching its "surprises" for the public. By insisting on the intricacies of private life, **nest** reveals the complete flattening of the public at the end of the 20th century.

    In its careful aversion of overt polemic, **nest** is a magazine in which the detonation charges often explode in snide asides. "Dawnridge makes Versailles look like a Comme des Garçons boutique. . . ." Skirting frivolity, flirting with seriousness, lapsing into earnestness and occasional self-righteousness, **nest**'s inventory of private utopias has the cumulative force of an implicit critique of all our current values. Overall, the spectacle is astonishing yet claustrophobic, like the explosion of a flashlight in a grotto that has never seen light before.

    I don't know a magazine today where word and image keep each other in such a dynamic balance. Texts "explain" images that seem otherwise incomprehensible, or words unlock the profound weirdness of seemingly innocent images.

    The breadth of **nest**'s "scanning" is overwhelming. No other magazine today has such a range—within its self-imposed, narrow focus on the interior. The effect is paradoxical—you want to interpret, or dream about a larger **nest**, a great general magazine that would combine cultural studies, anthropology, sociology, and even semiotics—but at the same time you realize its strength is its exclusive focus on a very narrow domain.

    While the level of the six **nest**'s is astounding, the variation between the issues is minimal; the same astonishing juxtapositions: insightful, pregnant anecdotes; suggestive, elliptical fairy tales; bombastic claims made for delicate works.

    That is where **nest**'s "design" kicks in—a curious hybrid of amateurism and calculation, its seeming arbitrariness a potent rebuke to current graphics, its "modernity"—like the four perforations in **nest** 6—an effective and radical vehicle to draw even the most seemingly regressive worlds or stories into the contemporary world.

    In an age where each magazine seems designed more to capture future investors than current readers, **nest** represents an aggressive, deliberate throwback to content, modulated with perfectly honed, contemporary pitch.

    You want many more **nest**s, but not **nest** forever. It is a corrective, a temporary breach, an opening...If **nest** is a manifesto, it is hoped that it will end, suddenly, like the Surrealists' reviews. Then it can assume its future status as legend.—*Rem Koolhaas*

BITCH LOUNGE

PHOTOGRAPHS NATHANIEL GOLDBERG
TEXT CARL SKOGGARD
CHAIR DESIGN TOM SACHS

JACQUES-LOUIS DAVID, PORTRAIT OF MME. RÉCAMIER, 1800. MUSÉE DU LOUVRE, PARIS.

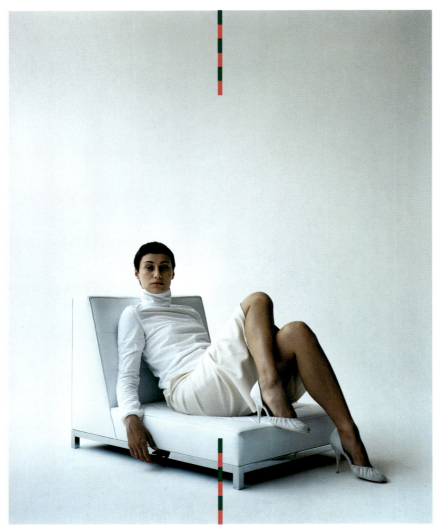

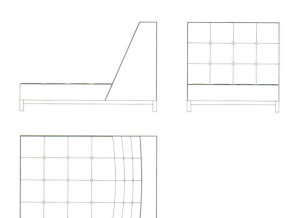

ELEVATIONS MICHAEL HENNES

nest was first shown a full-scale cardboard model of *Bitch Lounge* while visiting sculptor Tom Sachs's studio. We then arranged for it to be realized under the artist's supervision. The work employs a welded, chrome-plated steel base and tufted leather upholstery. Our text for "Bitch Lounge" (reprinted in full) launched itself on a comparison between *Bitch Lounge* and its French predecessor of two centuries ago. This feature led up ever so stealthily to an "ad"—one that does not seem to have raised a single honest customer, not yet at least.

The two great phyla of the furniture kingdom have always been at loggerheads. While chairs hold us upright and alert, priming us for social encounter, beds undo all our days, issuing their invitation to dream or dally.

Somewhere in between you have the couch. This invention was inevitable, if only to give seduction its due. Civilized passage to physical intimacy, delicious lingering on the threshold of abandon is caught perfectly in Jacques-Louis David's celebrated portrait of Madame Récamier. Glance a moment at the socially and sexually forward twenty-three-year-old posing at her ease yet with Pythagorean exactitude. How serenely she floats, toes winking, amid her antique accouterments.

Récamier's couch, designed by David himself, does not merely echo feminine aspirations. Raised high on impossible ballerina points, it stretches as gracefully as the young woman, quite extending her reach. Together they preside over one sheer, inexhaustible curve.

Alas, times change, and we with them. Several months ago sculptor Tom Sachs was inspired to create *Bitch Lounge*, occupied here by Renata Paris, a twenty-three-year-old Brazilian model of our acquaintance. *Bitch Lounge* is actually an anticouch. Barely higher off the floor than the humblest pallet, dauntingly dense as Corbu's misnomered "Grand Comfort" armchair, Sachs's piece curbs today's would-be bitch in every direction.

Unlike complacent Madame Récamier reclining full-length with room to spare, Renata is cruelly curtailed, obliged to draw in her legs and hunch her knees sharply. Even more distressing is her lowly altitude, which puts her at a comical disadvantage with others. The tiny feet of her chaise are heavylifting nowhere; she is trapped in a supergravitational field of her very own. Yet this squat piece of furniture is as much the collaborator as Récamier's attenuated sofa. *Bitch Lounge*, a bitch of a place in which to find yourself, goads its occupant to triumph over lowliness.

Renata understands, at least. Without instruction she has assumed the slightly strained position imagined by Tom Sachs, asserting hauteur in place of altitude. She cranes about, trying out vicious expressions, pleased to be on her paradoxical throne. She cradles against the subtle concavity of its back. One lissome arm waves this way and that before settling uneasily, like a garter snake, on the generous ledge behind her shoulders.

This is work, however: Récamier looks on, supremely placid, as her younger sister struggles to be all she can be. Will she achieve the contemporary ideal? Being a real bitch is not easy.

Eventually Renata gets up, leaving an empty station. It unsettles me, this intriguing, even handsome, object. Might it suit to display a becoming pair of fifty-three-year-old male thighs? Though prudence puts in a word, I am tempted.

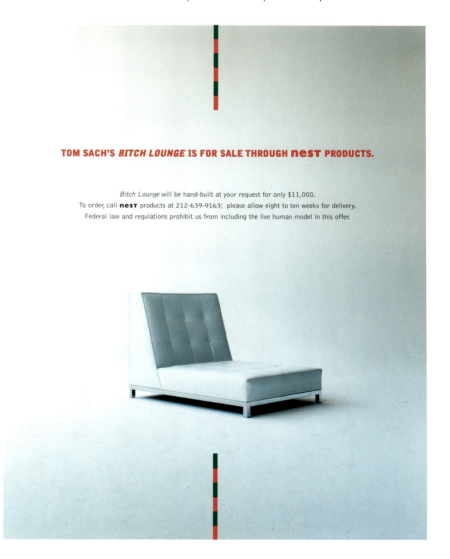

A FLIP BOOK

Humor is never far when you open an issue of **nest**. This ingredient, however, was particularly prominent in issue 8 (spring 2000). But why even open the magazine? Our covers, on which three stories incongruously met, said it all. Looming front and center was Tom Cary, a fabulously obscure collector of 1940s and 1950s bric-a-brac and the subject of our feature "The Dear Hunter." Behind him (actually, Cary and his cocktail trolley were a cutout applied with glue) sang the muted lyricism of Shigeru Ban's pine-invaded Japanese dacha ("A Wall-less House"). And on the rear cover was the same Japanese scene, enlivened by two camp Hollywood Egyptians we borrowed from the incredibly ancient Liz Taylor vehicle *Cleopatra*. (Inside, the two became bit players in "We're Rather Close," a serious feature about the Nile Valley tomb built for a pair of male manicurists just four thousand years ago.)

Readers were taking their chances with a "no nude issue," the front cover proclaimed, lower left. (After an alarmed staff member reported that every human form within these covers was clothed to one degree or another, we thought such an announcement **nest**'s responsibility.) Another box listed our near sweep of the 1999 Folio Awards. In the upper-right-hand corner (sheared with a die-cut) was the first of 107 images of a Matt Groening flipbook featuring Bender, hapless alcoholic automaton and a regular on Groening's weekly animated TV series *Futurama*. Meanwhile, utilitarian elements such as the bar code were strangely prominent or otherwise out of place. Taken altogether, with this cover we showed an information-rich though hardly sober front.

In **nest** 8 the up front story ("Please Leave the Room") was larger than before. Our editor's letter, lightly pondering the differences between art and decoration, led to its subject, namely, how much more interesting canonic artworks are without their human element. Holtzman's letter and three pages of pokerfaced "Please Leave the Room" lunacy have been included here.

Two more lighthearted features were "Pencil Case," about a San Francisco Victorian transformed by the relentless use of pencils and related paraphernalia as wall and ceiling décor (our typography seems to have been affected), and "Rooms for Sex," documenting theme rooms in S/M studios and swinger clubs across America. Apropos the latter: **nest** rarely shirks a patriotic duty.

"Grange à la Grange" took note of a rural French interior designed by Jacques Grange, whose skills as an architect and restorer were on view as well. Embellished with accolades to Grange elicited from other eminent decorators, the feature might have been read by a cynic as (c)overt promotion, but quite honestly, the thought never crossed **nest**'s mind. Before such a decorating talent we gape with admiration, *c'est tout*.

"Doll Lady" brought Mark Haven's exquisite unpublished images (1974) of an elderly Italian American named Mary and her tender inanimate charge, likewise a Mary. The remarkable thing about the two Maries was their utter lack of self-consciousness in front of a stranger's camera. We questioned members of the close-knit New York neighborhood where Mary the doll used to peer into the street from her second-floor window, yet learned little of the other Mary: These pictures are what is left of her.

Dearest Reader
(and dearest, *dearest* Subscriber),

I know the difference when I see it. But even if I stubbed my big toe on it, I would not really be able to explain it: the difference between art and decoration.

From the way people talk, you might imagine it is rather simple, that art is valuable and decoration, well, less so. "Artistic decoration" sounds like a compliment, while "decorative painting" is a put-down in almost everybody's lexicon. Sometimes I think art is for the big boys; it is just what it is, never apologizes, and absolutely forces you to say "Wow!" While decoration, supposedly, is deferential, content to serve something more important than itself. A flatterer.

Reader, when you find yourself riveted by the picture frame instead of the picture, that's your decorative impulse taking over. Only you mustn't be ashamed. Let others enjoy art while you identify with the artful. Embrace, whatever its cause, your decorative condition!

Everyone turns a hand to decorating now and then; some of us, however, are truly confirmed. Hard wiring could account for alarming cases like mine. I have a photographic recall for rooms and their objects, but faces and features make a fool of me. Don't invite Joe Holtzman to a movie where the same character reenters "disguised" in a different costume; he'll never make the connection.

When you come down to it, life itself is a mystery desperately in need of decoration. Even the big boys will never really get the big picture, but we decorators can make the edges look *so* good no one will much care.

Joseph Holtzman

P.S. On the following pages, certain famous paintings have been edited to save room freaks the trouble. (This is how we end up seeing them anyway.)

Joey Holtzman, in his room in his parents' house in Baltimore, as a virgin decorator. This photo was shot by his elder sister and nemesis, Lisa, a non-decorator (destined to become a crop-duster and emergency medical pilot).

107

JAMES ABBOTT MCNEILL WHISTLER, *Arrangement in Grey and Black*, also known as *Whistler's Mother*, oil on canvas, 1871 (Musée d'Orsay, Paris). A room inside the artist-decorator's London residence. The wall, framed by a low, stylish dado, has been glazed in several layers of various semitransparent pigments so as to achieve depth of tone. On it, *Black Lion Wharf*, an 1859 etching by Whistler, holds center stage. Even more attention-getting is the Japanese or Japanese-inspired silk embroidery (left), which functions here either as a wall curtain or portiere. What precious little we see of the slender, ebonized chair hints of Godwin; the upholstered footstool is of fumed oak.

108

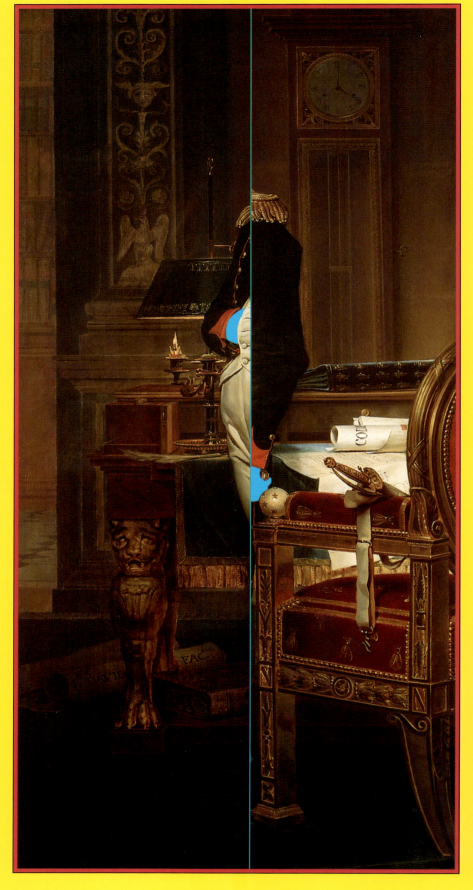

JACQUES-LOUIS DAVID, *Napoleon in His Study*, oil on canvas, 1812 (Louvre, Paris). A grandly austere Neoclassical setting. Viewers are inevitably thunderstruck by the Imperial Coronation chair (foreground), of giltwood with embroidered Lyons silk velvet upholstery, designed by Percier and Fontaine and in all likelihood realized by F.-H.-G. Jacob-Desmaltier, 1770-1841. A throne like it survives at the Chateau de Fontainebleau. Of particular interest are the appliquéd gold bees on the velvet and, on the armrests, those august ivory spheres mounted with gilt-bronze stars. Though in the background, the Empire long-case, key-wound clock, bouillote table lamp with guttering candles (a sentimental detail), and massive secretary with gilded griffin legs are also worthy of attention.

MASTER OF FLÉMELLE (ROGER CAMPIN?), *The Annunciation*, oil on wood, c. 1425-28 (The Cloisters, The Metropolitan Museum of Art, New York). This well-appointed room possesses both Romanesque and Gothic architectural elements. The long pine bench with footboard (left, partially obscured) has a back that pivots to allow sitters to face either the hearth or the room. It is ornamented with Gothic tracery and four lion finials, and draped in fine fabric—too fine to waste on the back side of the bench cushion. The adjustable metal sconces above the hearth as well as the floral decorated andirons (fire-dogs) are excellent examples of early 15th-century northern European metalwork. The blue-and-white towel hanging from the bracket on the back wall is linen and was a common Italian import of the period. In the window, delicate lattice-work of a wooden screen echoes lozenge patterns framing two family crests in the leaded glass above. The round trestle table—plainly the focus of this painting—has a collapsing top which is accommodated by the flat side of the table base. On the table are a blue-and-white majolica jug (tin-glazed Italian earthenware), brass candlestick, and leather-bound religious book with its green-and-red drawstring bag. The floor is covered in square and hexagonal glazed ceramic tiles.

JAN VAN EYCK, *Giovanni Arnolfini and His Wife*, oil on panel, 1434 (National Gallery, London). An upper-class Bruges interior of the 15th century, with characteristic twin windows. It is accoutered in what is known as "furniture of estate," associated with high social standing. The half-tester bed with its large pine headboard is upholstered in stamped or ferronie red velvet made of silk or wool. Its canopy would have hung by a system of chains (not visible here) from the ceiling beams. One of the bedcurtains has been tucked up into itself as a sacklike shape. Tragically, Van Eyck has allowed several intriguing pieces to remain partially hidden, among them the high-backed Gothic armchair next to the bed, topped with finials depicting griffins (on the seat) and Saint Margaret triumphing over the Dragon (on the seat back). A bench along the rear wall is draped in red fabric, wool perhaps, with matching cushions. The circular convex mirror above it is mounted in a wooden frame with ten rondels decorated with scenes from the Passion. Near it is suspended a string of amber beads adorned with silk fringes. The chandelier, of brass, is Flemish; the rug, of which we are granted a mere sliver (center right), is probably a Middle Eastern import of woven or knotted wool. The windowpanes are of crown glass, whose small, thick discs are the byproduct of a manufacturing process used since Roman times (in which a hollow metal rod is used to blow a glass bubble and then rotated rapidly, causing the bubble to flatten out as a sheet of glass).

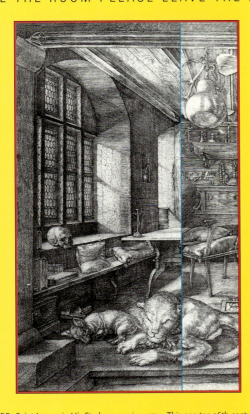

ALBRECHT DÜRER, *Saint Jerome in His Study*, engraving, 1514. This spartan 16th-century Germanic interior, remarkably like one of the upper rooms in Dürer's own house, is almost free of the usual annoying obstructions. The multi-paneled windows are, once again, of crown glass. Running along both the window wall and the rear wall is a simple unupholstered banquette, strewn with fat cushions. More striking are the quaintly proportioned chair with spindly, channeled legs and its companion table resting on splayed, unturned legs (homely pieces positively radiating spirituality). Finally, storage space for metal candlesticks and various earthenware or glass containers is offered by a high shelf. Pine, most likely, was the wood used for the sturdy joiner's furniture so carefully illustrated here. Such pieces may lack the sophisticated construction of later cabinetry but betray a craftsman's eye for harmony and shapely detail. The artist's monogram and the date of the engraving are displayed on a small pine tablet with leather hanging strap lying on the floor.

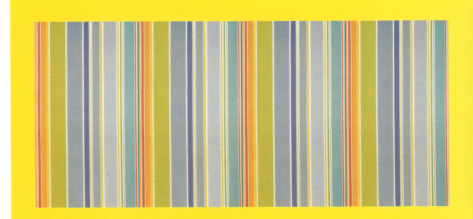

KENNETH NOLAND, *Summer Plain*, acrylic on canvas, 1967 (courtesy of William Doyle Galleries, New York). Here we have a provocative pattern that any adventurous interior designer will be delighted to employ as a repeat motif in wallpaper, upholstery fabric, etc. As with Noland's stripes, the decorative possibilities of such a pattern are truly endless.

PENCIL CASE

photographs RICHARD BARNES original text KIERA COFFEE

Please send pencil donations to: Jason Mecier, c/o Jaina Davis, P.O. Box 40608, San Francisco, CA 94140.

111

This feature documented an ongoing project for completely covering a three-story stairwell with murals fashioned mainly out of pencils. The artist Jason Mecier has made a name for himself with celebrity portraits using beans and noodles, matches and lighters, yarn, fake fingernails, etc. Once he chooses a material, it is explored until every limit is reached. "Pencil Case" was a borderline case for **nest**: Delighting in obsessive art, we remain unmoved by artless obsessions.

Following page (left): A prophetic portrait of Jaina Davis, commissioner of the murals. She has been made to look 50 years old, though at the time of the portrait she would admit to only 30. What will she and it look like in 20 years?

Grange à la Grange

photographs Jean-Louis Garnell
original text Paul B. Franklin

This page and following four pages: The ultimate yield of Jacques Grange's creative effort is harmony, and objects contributing to the effect need not be striking or precious. This decorator "invites his clients to feel comfortable with being comfortable," our writer, Paul B. Franklin, shrewdly observed. "In a culture where the ceremoniousness of *l'art de vivre* is sacrosanct, Grange's aesthetic philosophy has attracted a surprising cadre of adherents." Merely the serenity and completeness of his rooms made **nest** feel so comfortable that we dispensed with captions. We just wanted to keep looking.

Photographs Katharina Bosse, *Operating Room* and *Classroom*, 1999, from the series "Realms of Signs, Realms of Senses"

Above and opposite page: "Rooms for Sex" taught us that for-profit sex chambers which propose a theme are dead set on being ordinary. Their authority rests in conformity to type, in not forgetting the bland detail. Your excitement would be ruined if you could sense another personality at work in them; even a convincing simulation of the stereotype might be unnerving, the begging of an unwanted question. From photographs we only know what does not go on here. Hudson himself said: "Thinking of these rooms as private residences, and perhaps shared with friends, cracked my smile."

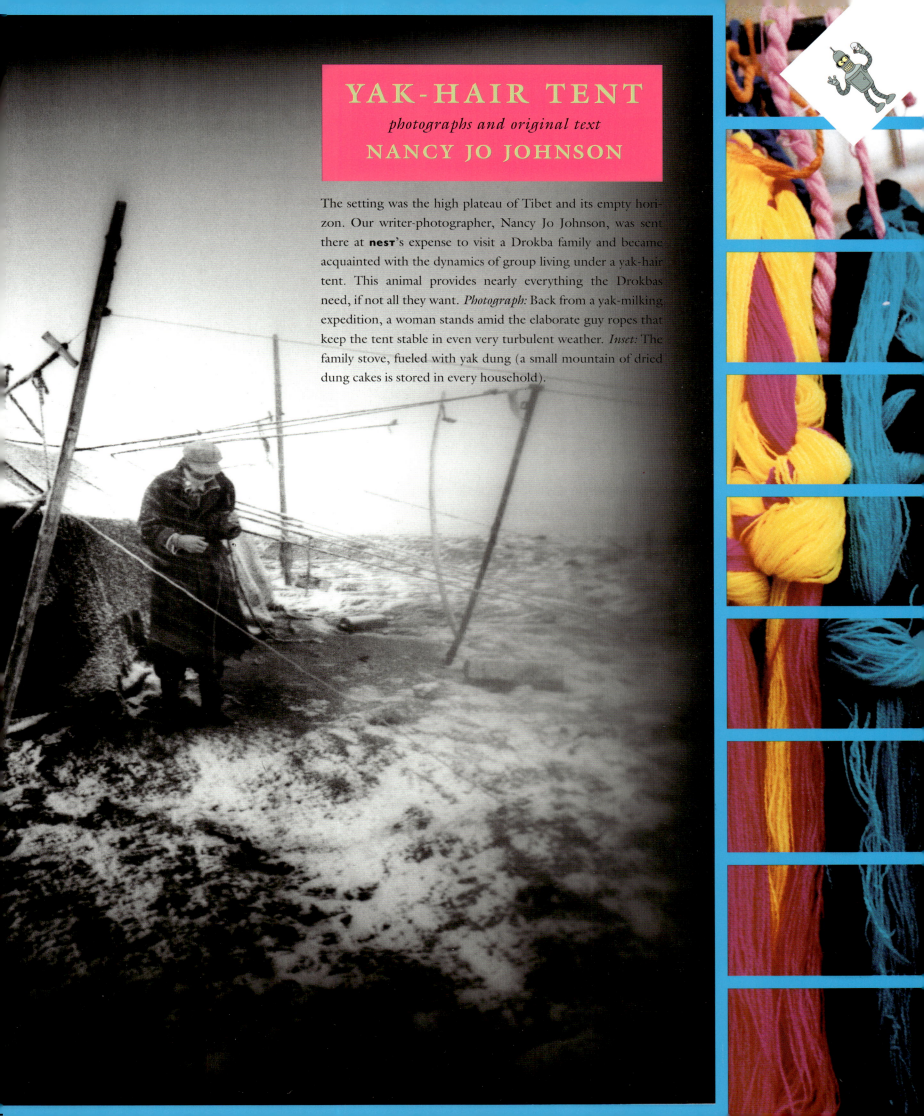

YAK-HAIR TENT

photographs and original text

NANCY JO JOHNSON

The setting was the high plateau of Tibet and its empty horizon. Our writer-photographer, Nancy Jo Johnson, was sent there at **nest**'s expense to visit a Drokba family and became acquainted with the dynamics of group living under a yak-hair tent. This animal provides nearly everything the Drokbas need, if not all they want. *Photograph:* Back from a yak-milking expedition, a woman stands amid the elaborate guy ropes that keep the tent stable in even very turbulent weather. *Inset:* The family stove, fueled with yak dung (a small mountain of dried dung cakes is stored in every household).

BROOME
ONE WAY
TOW-AWAY ZONE
NO PARKING
8AM-9AM
EXCEPT SUNDAY
1/2 HOUR PARKING
9AM-7PM
EXCEPT SUNDAY
PUBLIC TELEPHONE

DOLL LADY

photographs MARK HAVEN original text MAUREEN HOWARD

These pages and following two pages: The Doll Lady—her name was Mary Pantalione—lived in Little Italy in lower Manhattan. Each day her doll, Mary, would take up its place in the window above Broome Street. The idea of a lone elderly woman making so much of a doll put off writer Maureen Howard at first, but her feelings shifted. "This is not Arbusland," she concluded, "it is simply their home. The photos are intimate, not intrusive. Doll and woman are neither spectacle, nor spectacular. The woman has given herself (and Mary) to the photographer without masquerade. They go about their business. The only dress-up is literal, getting the child properly dressed for the picture."

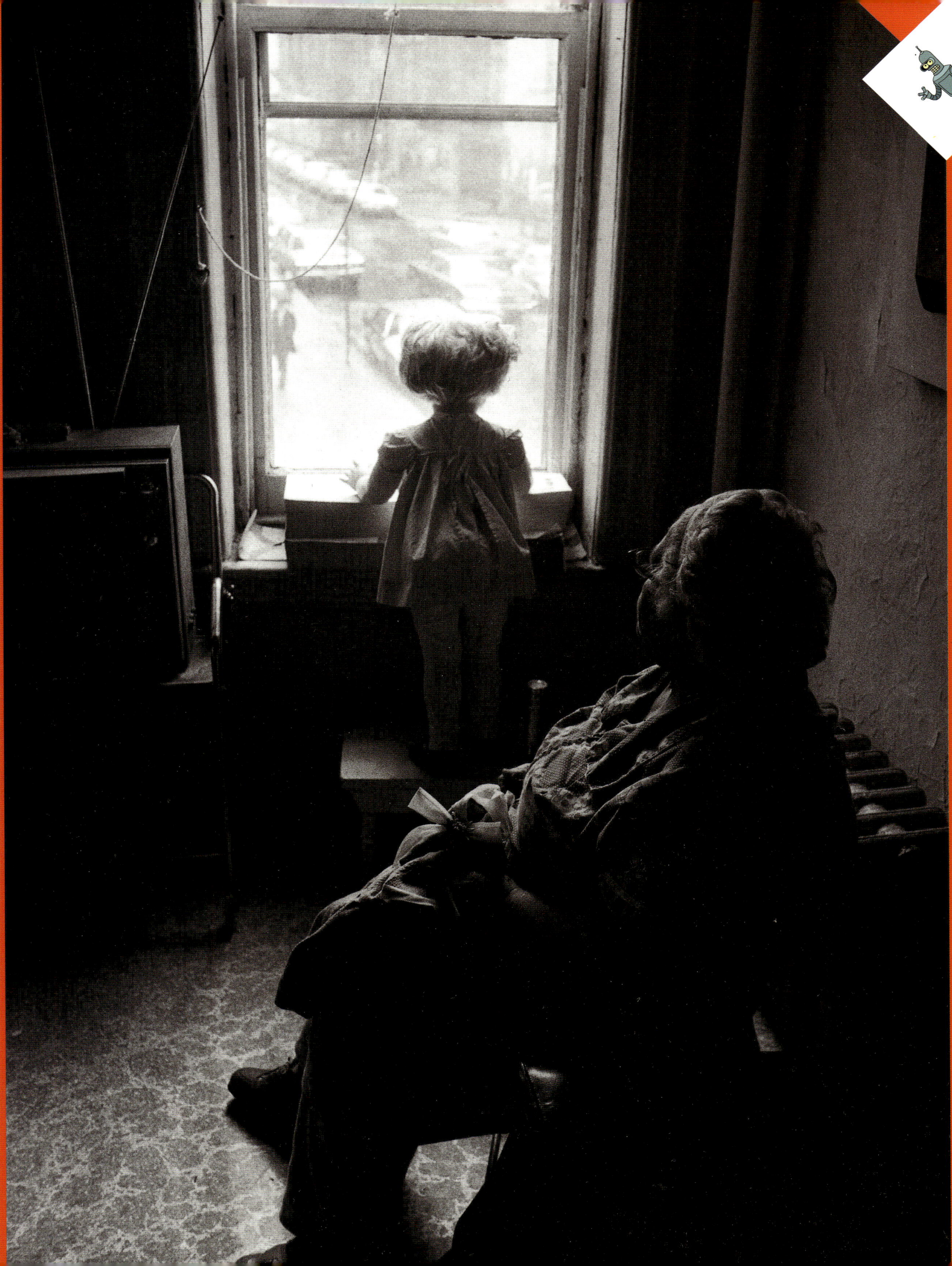

QUESTION OF DECENCY

After the refreshing "all no nude issue," nudity reared an ugly and unrepentant head immediately in **nest** 9 (summer 2000). Two young people wearing scratch-off swimwear designed for us by Todd Oldham occupied the front and rear covers. It was up to readers whether to scratch or not. If they did, frank nudity awaited. My 83-year-old mother scratched, and curiosity satisfied, restored her covers to decency by making her own little suits for the new Adam and Eve (but whatever one did, those snakes were hatching from eggs inside the **nest** logo).

Actually the cover couple *were* Adam and Eve, inasmuch as they were spending five days and nights in our Garden of Eden, a midtown Manhattan hotel room tricked out with plastic fruits and flowers, colored lights, etc. Their sojourn in this snug paradise generated some intriguing up front pages, where, in deference to historical accuracy, **nest** did not permit any fig leaves. A rather wistful report was filed from location by (the definitively post-Edenic) Tobias Schneebaum. Our innocent pair, we later learned, had been in between apartments at the time, so their hotel interlude came as a real boon.

Issues of dress and undress were also tackled elsewhere in **nest** 9. Two beleaguered colonies from the 1950s, nudists and cross-dressers, practically collided. Images of the former, borrowed from old-fashioned nudist magazines in which people play squash and canasta in the altogether, were used for our contributor and subscription pages. A suburban coterie of cross-dressing men in the Mamie Eisenhower taste was rescued from oblivion thanks to a cache of hundreds of photographs found by friends of **nest** in a flea market ("Casa Susanna"). If nudists gained an identity only by shucking their garments, cross-dressers would have felt absolutely naked without theirs.

Very few decorators practice in the old way—still popular with **nest**—where each element of a room is custom-designed according to a comprehensive scheme. But everything in the whimsical Paris bedroom we showed in "Conjuring the Elements with Garouste and Bonetti" had been created for the occasion. The result was like someone's dream in which all the details make mysterious sense. Editor-in-chief Joseph Holtzman introduced the feature by comparing Garouste and Bonetti with William Chippendale, another favorite decorator.

No survey of **nest** 9 could afford to omit its excursions into the psychology of collecting, a topic always close to our heart. "An Unruly Passion for Things" permitted a man of the cloth, Peter J. Gomes of Harvard University, to ponder object-love in light of the Scriptures. His text was inserted into the issue in small pamphlet format—an allusion to his calling. More fire but less light was given off by "I Cannot Imagine My Life Without the Collection of Gas Welding Torches," an account of accumulating in Liguria submitted by Fulvio Ferrari. "Have I ever," Ferrari asked himself, "used any of the dozens of hammers or the eight champagne buckets, the device for making rope by hand, or the wooden or plastic lasts for fabricating shoes?" If you ask us: An honest man had better not try and explain his passions.

nest **A QUARTERLY OF INTERIORS**

$12.50 SUMMER 2000

0 75470 64633 1   02>

exclusive swimwear by Todd Oldham may be scratched off at your own risk

Cover photographs Nathaniel Goldberg; **nest** logo photograph Manny Rubio

nest commissioned landscape architect Ken Smith to design this plastic garden, which he installed in Room 401 of the Roger Smith Hotel in mid-Manhattan. (We have very little against gardens, as long as they are inside.) A good dimensional sense of the room could be gained from our two covers, which showed opposing pairs of walls. To make sure readers got it, Adam and Eve held the same pose for each shot.

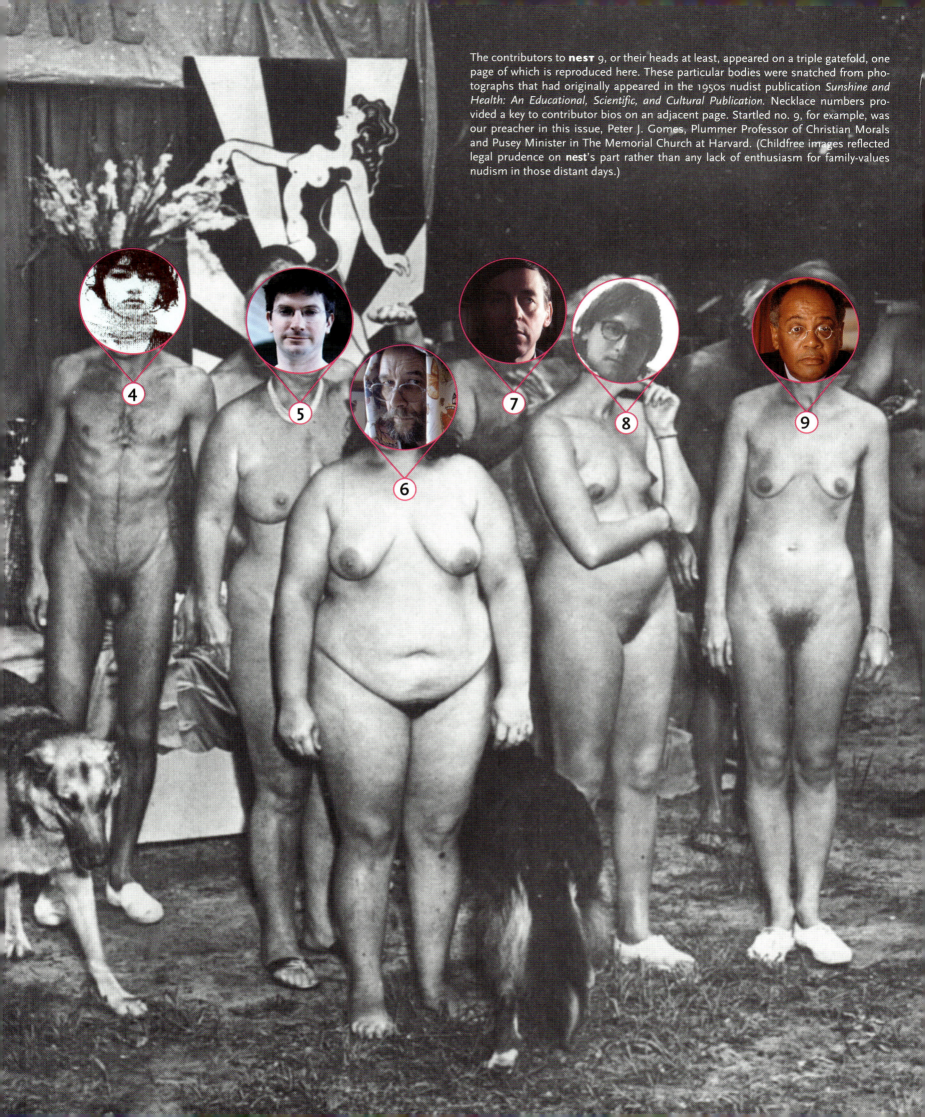

The contributors to **nest** 9, or their heads at least, appeared on a triple gatefold, one page of which is reproduced here. These particular bodies were snatched from photographs that had originally appeared in the 1950s nudist publication *Sunshine and Health: An Educational, Scientific, and Cultural Publication*. Necklace numbers provided a key to contributor bios on an adjacent page. Startled no. 9, for example, was our preacher in this issue, Peter J. Gomes, Plummer Professor of Christian Morals and Pusey Minister in The Memorial Church at Harvard. (Childfree images reflected legal prudence on **nest**'s part rather than any lack of enthusiasm for family-values nudism in those distant days.)

Advertisers often insist on their copy appearing next to an editorial page rather than another ad. The synergy between our present up front pages and the fashion ads they were designed to face—between the placidly naked and the creepily clothed—was often wonderful. This pair of images also illustrates the strange effect of the die-cut used in issue 9: Once the magazine was lying open before you, it foreshortened towards the top and proposed an ultimate convergence of seemingly parallel lines.

130

Photograph Nathaniel Goldberg

Prada Tel +1 888 977 1900

PRADA

CONJURING
THE ELEMENTS
WITH GAROUSTE
AND BONETTI

Describing a Paris bedroom designed by Garouste and Bonetti, we must have been mugged by fancy. "Evidently fire and water contend here," one caption read. The bed was "really" a flaming pyre and all this wavering furniture an emanation of the center rug's fiery energies. Or did one piece beget the next? Could the kidney-shaped dressing table (following two pages) be "dream-kin" to the curled-fern valance above? It was quite a trip.

photographs
JEAN-LOUIS GARNELL

I CANNOT IMAGINE MY LIFE WITHOUT THE COLLECTION OF GAS WELDING TORCHES

PHOTOGRAPHS GIORGIO JANO   ORIGINAL TEXT FULVIO FERRARI

A cluster of five-hundred-year-old stone houses perched high above the Mediterranean was the setting for Fulvio Ferrari's "I Cannot Imagine My Life Without the Collection of Gas Welding Torches." Ferrari, a pioneering dealer in modern and contemporary Italian design, has taught the world to esteem and value what he passionately loves, and is one of nest's loyal supporters. At his weekend house in Verezzi, near Genoa, he shares with visitors his enthusiasm for local wines and other components of the good life as practiced in his neighborhood. A firm faith in regional culture came out when Ferrari wrote about the unlabeled bottles that appear on his table: "The wine comes from 'Beppe and the mules' or Romano Rembado. Or it could be from the *pigato* grape of Aracà. I hate standardized bottles of wine that have undergone filtration, pasteurization, and all those things required by the Office of Hygiene. My wines can be turbid, they have delicate and cloudy sediments, and are true and alive with the flavor of flowers and sea air."

The country house of Fulvio Ferrari is well stocked with objects both refined and rude. "How could I," he asked of no one in particular, "do without the big iron eighteenth-century bell tower clock mechanism which—marvelous coincidence—comes from Ormea, the town where I was born? Without the fifty bobbin-shaped bronze weights that belong to balances of the Republic of Genoa, once capital of the world because of its commercial wealth, which I like to think was balanced by my ancient weights? Without the prototypes of the chandeliers designed by Toni Cordero and fabricated so painstakingly by my friends, the Del Campos, a family of enamelists? Without the Sottsass Asteriods standing since 1984 on the credenza and illuminating the living room with their pink and blue plastic lights?"

In our magazine version, the double gatefold reproduced here (top) was followed by the triple one (bottom). Together they created a 5-page gatefold (middle). Pullout pages allowed us to really show off the 360° panoramic shots made with Giorgio Jano's camera. The instrument rotates at whatever speed suits the conditions of ambient light, the only light which Jano uses. When outdoor and indoor space appear in a single image, it is necessary to take advantage of the moment in which the balance between the two sources of light is perfect. Thus Jano can take only one such image per day.

AN UNRULY PASSION

for

THINGS

by

PETER J. GOMES★

photographs

DERRY MOORE

I cannot remember a time when I was not interested in things and in their arrangement. For all of my sentient life I have entered a room and rearranged it according to my fancy and, alas, I tend to judge people at first sight, not upon their manner, physical appearance, or the quality of their discourse, but rather on how they arrange the space in which they live. Even before advertising copy seized upon it, I had always believed in the fatality of the slogan, "You have only one opportunity to make a first impression"; and for me, a spiritual man trapped in a material world, that first impression has to do with the way in which space is organized, shapes and textures are arranged, and colors punctuate.

Where does such an obsession begin? In my case it didn't come from my family, for though as a child I was always fascinated by other people's houses and their rooms, my father was a sensible farmer who spent more time outdoors than indoors, and my mother was a musician with a strong aesthetic sense. My father was a very good gardener with a fascination for the lawn and for beautifully trimmed hedges; he was a terror on weeds, and he knew nature's seasons and her rituals as only an outdoors man can, but he had no interest whatsoever in the interior landscape. My mother, on the other hand, a preacher's daughter, had her mind on the beautiful and the spiritual, yet was hardly house-proud.

When I was a child, in the 1940s, my mother was forced to work in other people's houses because, as she would say, we weren't poor, we just didn't have enough money; so, often to the distress of my father, she offered her services to the well-to-do to supplement the family exchequer. Fortunately, her friends were well-connected and she helped the local good and the great, and sometimes she would take me along with her. Thus, at an early age I came to see some of the splendid houses of our area. Many of the families for whom she worked, and their establishments, were already in a state of decline, the old money that had supported them beginning to run out. It was in those old Yankee houses that I discovered what would later be called the "shabby gentility of the prosperous classes," which included worn old Zuber French wallpapers, threadbare Oriental rugs, streaked family portraits with chipped gesso frames, vast collections of mended rose-medallion and Canton china, and the general

★*Plummer Professor of Christian Morals and*
Pusey Minister in The Memorial Church, Harvard University

effect of houses well lived-in whose essentially good bones wore well the ravages of time and neglect. I knew instinctively that such a "look" could never be achieved by the most zealous of decorators or collectors, for such places were the accumulation of generations of mixed tastes and abilities, the whole of which was greater than the sum of its parts. To this day I associate the smell of old boxwood, furniture polish, and damp with those places of childhood fantasy. Sad to say, none of them survive except in my imagination, although perhaps I have spent my adult life trying to recreate them in the two houses in which I have the privilege of living today.

Mine was not an entirely blank aesthetic slate upon which to write, a point my late mother would hasten to make. We had "things" with good lines and interesting provenances. Some pieces of silver and a set of well-turned Irish sherry glasses that sat upon our sideboard, I was told, had been "liberated" from the Virginia plantation house from which some of my maternal ancestors had fled at the time of their emancipation during the Civil War. In addition to these things there were a pair of fine water goblets and some table linen that had belonged to some of our New England ancestors from the Congdon Street neighborhood of Providence, Rhode Island, which we used only at Thanksgiving and on solemn family occasions. A Victorian chest of drawers was said also to have come from Virginia. How it could possibly have arrived up north I do not know, but I never questioned the legitimacy of the story and, as it is mine, I cherish its physical link, real or imagined, with my ancestors.

During my high-school years I worked as a janitor both after school and in the summers, in one of Plymouth's historic house museums. Built in the 1740s, the house had been lived in by the same family until the death of the last male descendant, James Spooner, a bachelor, who had died just a few years before I began to work there. The Spooners had been among Plymouth's premier merchant families, and apparently had never thrown anything away. Fortunately, in addition to a natural parsimony they had also had good taste and the money to indulge it, and hence the house was a trove of good stuff— nothing ostentatious in the fashion of the Newport gilded age, but the accumulation of three centuries of local gentry. I was instructed in the fine art of particular housekeeping by Mr. Spooner's last housekeeper, Ida, a redoubtable Nova Scotian woman with a sharp eye and a sharper tongue. Mr. Spooner had left his house to be exhibited as a museum, but as his housekeeper pointed out, he would be horrified at the bobtail and rabble who for the price of admission felt at liberty to put grimy fingerprints on the polished copper splashboard in the kitchen, manipulate the leather-bound books in the library, and try to squeeze polyester-clad bottoms into wing chairs and onto sofas. Keeping the house fit for visitors, most of whom Mr. Spooner would have never admitted, was a hard and demanding task, but Ida and I regarded it as a game, a conspiracy of "us" against "them."

At about this time, and perhaps inspired by my job in Mr. Spooner's house, I began to frequent the local antique shops. One of them was far and above the most interesting of the shops in town, largely because its long-time owner, Hyman Klasky, was not just a dealer in furniture but a European-trained cabinetmaker of the first order. He was a Jew, born and trained in Russia who, early in the century, had fled his homeland and the terrible anti-Semitism of late-tsarist Russia. He ended up in New England after a series of adventures. As a young immigrant Mr. Klasky worked as a carver and joiner for Irving and Casson, the great furniture and woodworking firm located in Cambridge, whose projects included Theodore Roosevelt's White House, Shepley Bulfinch's Memorial Church at Harvard, the new Boston Public Library, and H.H. Richardson's fabulous Trinity Church. Klasky had worked on the last two himself, as an apprentice to one of the most remarkable woodcarvers of his day, John—or Johannes—Kyrchmayer.

When I came upon Hyman Klasky he had long been settled in Plymouth, and had established his shop and reputation over many years. When he learned that I had been admitted into Bates College, he told me with some pride that one of his first jobs was as an apprentice carver to Mr. Kyrchmayer, who had executed the chancel furnishings in the Bates College Chapel. The gentry of Plymouth were delighted to find a master craftsman in their midst, one who could repair the odd clock or highboy, and Mr. Klasky's business began as some house-poor Yankees would pay him with a piece of furniture or two. He became an expert in restoration, an appraiser in whom the banks and courts had confidence, and often the means through which the old families sold off their goods and chattel. When the great Israel Sack made his periodic forays throughout New England, scavenging for the insatiable New York market, he considered no trip complete without a side visit to Plymouth and to Klasky, who kept a mental inventory of every worthwhile piece in every house in the vicinity.

I was still in high school when I ventured into his shop and nervously looked around. I knew that the shop was no place for a young man with no money, but I also knew that I was enchanted by the splendid disarray, the art of the craftsman, and the sense that beauty and history commingled higgledy-piggledy on the shop's premises. I was terrified that I would be asked either to buy something, or to leave; while I was asked neither, Mr. Klasky did want to know who I was and why I was in his shop. I told him that I worked in Mr. Spooner's house, and that unleashed from Mr. Klasky a torrent of anecdote and a recital of practically everything of note in the Spooner house. After I discovered that he liked to talk I visited him whenever I could, and I asked questions until eventually I screwed up enough courage to ask the price of a fine-looking Hepplewhite sideboard. I think now that it may have been a centennial piece, beautifully made in the 1870s. "You've got good taste but no money," Mr. Klasky said, not dismissively but factually. I ventured into the large area devoted to picture frames and mirrors, and there I found a small painting on board of a flower in a vase. I was intrigued more by the frame than by the painting, a simple but handsome gilt frame like so many in the Spooner house. I asked how much it was. Mr. Klasky thought for a few minutes, calculating, I supposed, his margin of profit, and he said, "Ten dollars." That was in 1957, and ten dollars was a lot of money for a high-school boy saving up his one-dollar-an-hour salary for college. I hesitated, but we both knew that I had to have it. "How much money have you?" he asked. I looked in my wallet, found that I had about three dollars, and leapt to the conclusion that he was a nice man who, taking pity on me, might give me the painting for that sum. I was partly right. "Give me two dollars now and a dollar a week, and you can have it," he said, "but you can't have it until it's paid for." Thus I made my first deal and bought my first piece, and I have it still: it hangs on the wall in the guest room in Sparks House, and I will never part with it.

Mr. Klasky and his son and successor in the business, Melvin Klasky, became my tutors and, in certain cases, my financiers, as I ventured into the avocation of acquisition. The elder Mr. Klasky is now long dead and the business is in the hands of Melvin, himself nearly, but fortunately not yet, retired. We have always joked about going into business together, but Melvin's father had once warned me that I would never succeed in the antique business. "Why?" I asked. "Because," he said, "you will buy only what you like, and then you won't want to part with it." I was cursed with an unruly passion for things, and would never be able to profit from it.

There have been times when my passion and my profession have seemed to be in conflict. I am a clergyman: I believe in invisible and impossible things, and the founder of my religion encouraged his followers to forsake the world and to follow him. The distinction between the material and the spiritual is always made in favor of the spiritual; and simplicity of life, traveling light through this veil of tears, is the compass of my faith. When Jesus says, "Lay not up for yourselves treasures upon earth, where moth and rust doth corrupt, and where thieves break through and steal...," he is speaking to people like me who are tempted to hoard beautiful things and direct attention to them rather than to God. "For where your treasure is," he says, "there will your heart be also." (Matthew 6:19, 21)

Yet the world-denying believer must confront the world-affirming creator, the one who makes beauty and order and invests his creatures with a love of such things. Taste may be merely our way of trying to restore something of what we lost when Eve, our mother, ate us out of house and home by taking that first bite from the forbidden fruit. Collecting is in some sense an act of creation: indeed, we are constantly recreating our environment, shaping the space in which we live, imposing a little order and beauty upon a world more familiar with ugliness and disorder. And in collecting we recreate not only our space, but ourselves. Not only do we bring other people's things into our world and make them, however temporarily, our own, but we are also possessed by that which we possess and seek; and thus does the past live, recreated by our hands. Collecting is the ultimate redistribution of wealth and beauty, accomplished not by a revolution nor by a cultural decree but by the ability of one generation to receive that which belonged to another. It pleases me to realize that some of the things that have found their way into my houses over the years would have been totally unavailable to me in their original settings in time and place. In what is regarded by many Philistines as an elitist pastime there is an inherent democracy, even a hint of socialism, suggesting rather clearly that aesthetics has no political ideology.

Collectors are peculiar people; I have always known that. Why we are, however, was never made clear to me until I was given, and read, *Collecting: An Unruly Passion*, a so-called psychological perspective by practicing psychoanalyst Werner Muensterberger (Princeton, 1994). In an analysis of collectors, many of whom are now long dead, Muensterberger does for collecting what Freud did for sex, telling us far more than we need or want to know, including that a collector is one who prefers things to people; a collector is one who tries to replace with things certain missing paternal and maternal instincts; collecting is fetishistic, anal, neurotic; and the collector a specimen as worthy of study as the things that he or she collects — and so forth. The person who gave me this book for Christmas either hadn't read it or, having done so, was trying to tell me something. One cannot really make sense of one's passions—which is why they are passions—but a helpful observation has put mine into some perspective for, early in the book, Muensterberger suggests:

> Thus, by searching for objects and, with any luck, discovering and
> obtaining them, the passionate collector combines his own re-created
> past consoling experiences with the fantasied past of his objects, in an
> almost mystical union.

Here, at least, I know what he's talking about.

CAPTIONS

For **nest**, Rev. Peter J. Gomes assumed his "Country Life pose" before a marble fireplace in the double parlor of his Plymouth, Massachusetts, home. The Lodge has long served him as a primary residence and a refuge from the clamor of university life.

Another shot of Gomes's double parlor, arrayed in Anglo-American taste. (Images for the Gomes feature were set against pattern backgrounds borrowed by **nest** from fabrics depicted in old religious paintings in Sydney Vacher's *Fifteenth-Century Italian Ornament*, 1886).

Some time ago, while at a New York flea market, we discovered a large collection of snapshots: album after aged album of neatly preserved images, taken roughly between the mid-fifties and mid-sixties, depicting a group of cross-dressers united around a house called Casa Susanna. The location: a rather large and charmingly banal Victorian-style house in a small town in New Jersey. The Girls used it as a weekend headquarters for a regular "girl's life." Someone, probably Susanna—the matriarch, the Star—nailed a wooden board on a tree proclaiming it "Casa Susanna," and thus a Queendom was born.

As could be expected, Susanna and her friends performed with regularity at drag shows, to which countless glamour photos, also found, bear witness. We discarded these photos to concentrate on the images of

the more private and intimate life at Casa Susanna. The Girls sweep the front porch, cook, knit, play scrabble, bathe in the nearby lake and, of course, dress. And how they dress! It is no longer for the glamour of the stage but for each other, as normal women would dress, albeit with their own sense of style. There is an evident pleasure of living here, a liberation, a simplification of the conflicts inherent in a double life.

The present collection of photographs is a digest of four hundred such images. Altogether they depict a cohesive story of a group of people seeking their freedom. We hope this door ajar into their universe will give you the same pleasure it gave us. Doesn't Susanna, after all these years, deserve the star treatment she so obviously relished, even if for reasons different from what she might have imagined? Can we dream?

text **MICHEL HURST** *and* **ROBERT SWOPE**

REDEEMING FEATURES

Recent issues of **nest** have grown more thematic, with decorative motifs and ideas beginning to percolate through whole volumes. **nest** 10 (fall 2000) turned to the decorator P-words: plaids and plastic, and their unholy offspring, plaid plastic slipcovers. The issue itself arrived in a zipped, see-through plastic bag in soft primary colors (reddish front, bluish back, edged in yellow). The plaids on the front cover and the brick pattern (a species of plaid) on the rear were, of course, visible even when the issue was "slipcovered," as our ever fanciful editor-in-chief, Joseph Holtzman, liked to imagine matters with his plastic zip bag.

Inside, Holtzman got down to business in the editor's letter, pumping for plaid plastic slipcovers. Readers were being softened up for a truly shocking up front story, "Patterns for Slatterns," which showed how an all-white 1970s Fire Island beach house could be "redeemed" with slipcovers and floor coverings of woven plaid patterned plastic. Even Robin Byrd herself—irredeemable diva of late-night New York cable and proprietor of the beach house in question—was recovered in a thatched plastic frock designed for her by John Bartlett. (Many other features in issue 10 were decorated with plaids, too).

Perhaps the only common denominator for "Excessively So: The Rothschilds at Waddesdon Manor" and "House for a Poet" was the color red; these two items staked out opposite poles of **nest**'s universe. In the first, decorator David Mlinaric contemplated French style at its daunting best with the eyes of a wised-up Anglo-Saxon (he had helped restore Waddesdon Manor and reinstall its superb collection of French furnishings). The second celebrated a radically simple New Age desert dwelling erected in New Mexico by the artist Richard Tuttle and his wife, poet Mei-mei Berssenbrugge. For the occasion, wraithlike poems by

her were married to sober photos of site-specific furnishings designed by him. The whole was then arranged in a novel layout whose red (**nest**'s custom blend) bled through the page as another ghostly element.

More P-words, patriotism and presidential election, may have had a share in our recreation of Louis Comfort Tiffany's décor for the Blue Room of the White House, completed in 1882 ("Presidential Blues"). Experts were hired to determine its hues (no contemporary color renderings have survived), and a cultural context for so signal an event in decorating history was suggested by Mary W. Blanchard, author of *Oscar Wilde's America: Counterculture in the Gilded Age.* Then there was "Navy Submarine," which took readers along on a nuclear sub's three-month patrol. This feature, continuing to sound the patriotic note, attended to the psychology and practicalities of an especially remote home environment and found decoration where very few had looked before. (Getting the U.S. Navy onboard the story was not the easiest thing we've ever done.)

Each issue of **nest** finishes up with a "final nest." Our original idea was to pay tribute to the sheer diversity of places in which each and every one of us will spend so much of our time, by-and-by. As **nest** issues come and go, however, this department is growing metaphorical. "Adult Baby," our final nest item for issue 10, saw us hooked up with Dave, a respectably employed 40-year-old going on two who liked to think of himself as "Daybee." We were able to respect Daybee's anonymity without denying readers' curiosity concerning his elaborately outfitted home nursery, where he sleeps in a man-sized crib and pees in man-sized diapers. Our writer, Kiera Coffee, managed as well to shed light on the adult baby community, which is putting down roots via the Internet.

Above: The zippered plastic cover for **nest** 10. *Photograph Eric Piasecki*

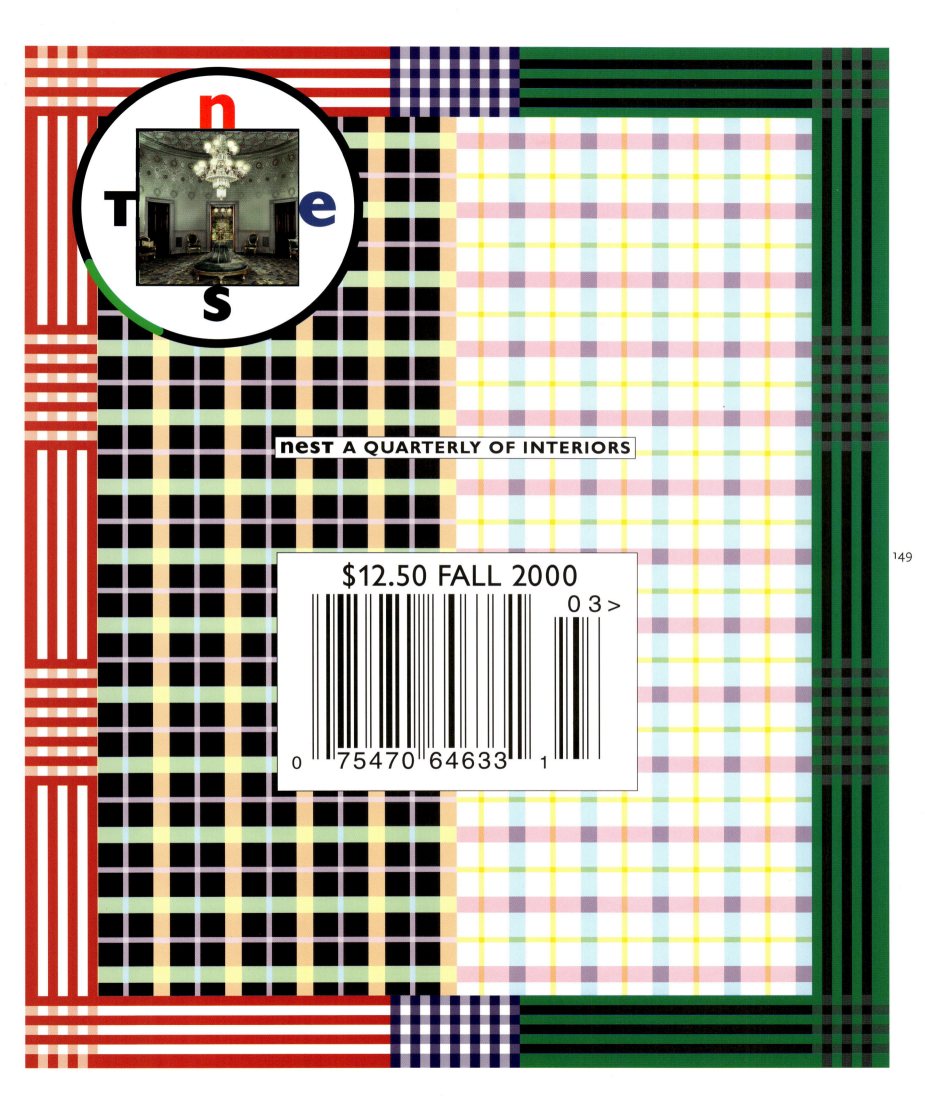

nest A QUARTERLY OF INTERIORS

$12.50 FALL 2000

0 3 >

0   75470 64633   1

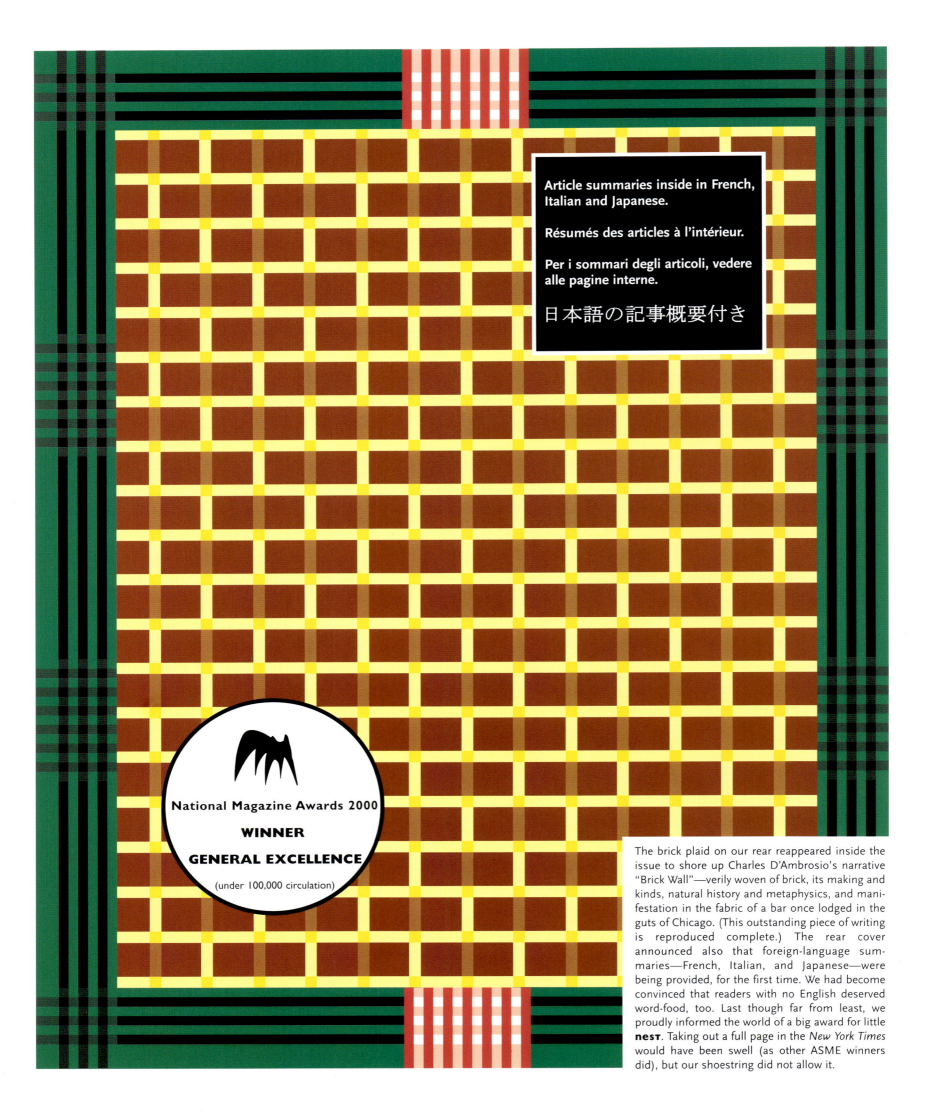

Article summaries inside in French, Italian and Japanese.

Résumés des articles à l'intérieur.

Per i sommari degli articoli, vedere alle pagine interne.

日本語の記事概要付き

National Magazine Awards 2000
WINNER
GENERAL EXCELLENCE
(under 100,000 circulation)

The brick plaid on our rear reappeared inside the issue to shore up Charles D'Ambrosio's narrative "Brick Wall"—verily woven of brick, its making and kinds, natural history and metaphysics, and manifestation in the fabric of a bar once lodged in the guts of Chicago. (This outstanding piece of writing is reproduced complete.) The rear cover announced also that foreign-language summaries—French, Italian, and Japanese—were being provided, for the first time. We had become convinced that readers with no English deserved word-food, too. Last though far from least, we proudly informed the world of a big award for little **nesт**. Taking out a full page in the *New York Times* would have been swell (as other ASME winners did), but our shoestring did not allow it.

PATTERNS FOR SLATTERNS   Robin Byrd modeling the thatched plastic number made for her at **nest**'s request by John Bartlett. In a note, Bartlett explained his choice of a basket-weave construction and a Polynesian pareo look, and confessed to being a "wide-eyed Midwestern fan of Ms. Byrd's unapologetic, liberating approach to human sexuality." *Following page (left):* A living room lineup of Byrd's formerly white chairs, together with a floorcloth, also in woven plastic (a caption clued in readers about this long-running cheap substitute for pile carpets, and advocated its revival in the shiny, transparent, easy-to-clean material we used for ours). From now on the up front story would give off a scholarly sheen, sort of. "Patterns for Slatterns" offered slightly potted histories of the slipcover and Scottish tartans—the latter turning out to be something of an exposé of wishful tartan history. *Photographs Nathaniel Goldberg*

152

Memory of the witnesses, a domestic space such as
origin in the present, is riddled with holes.

The light is so close I can't catch it through ourselves it
shines through.

HOUSE
FOR
A
POET

This page and the following three pages: **nest** joined the poetry of Mei-mei Berssenbrugge with photos of furniture designed by her husband, the artist Richard Tuttle, for their desert New Mexico home. Her wisps of poetry and his solid snaps were held in place by mysterious eruptions of red—which became rose ghosts on each reverse side of the special lightweight paper we used for the feature.

When the scene is complex, I turn to the audience and comment
outloud, then return to the room and language at hand,
weakened by whoever couldn't hear me, as if I don't recognize
the room, because my family moved in when I was away.

157

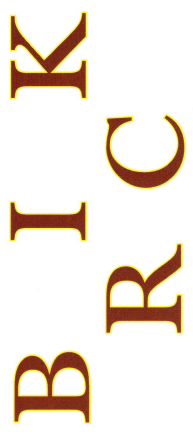

Charles D'Ambrosio

Now what remains of the place is an anonymous wall of brick, but not so long ago my uncle ran a bar at 112-1/2 Clinton Street, the half being our family's share in the City of Big Shoulders, Chicago. If the Sears Tower were considered the gnomon of a sundial, and you were inclined to tell time by organizing shadows, then the bar was located at roughly ten o'clock in the morning. By midmorning the shadows swept in, the air darkened and the streets turned silty, creating sunken rivers of early night, murky and unpromising to most people but suiting just fine the shady temper of the hardcore drinkers and gamblers the bar catered to. In fact they came precisely for that halfness, that demimonde aspect of the address. The building itself occupied an alley that had formerly served as a cattle-run from the trains to the stockyards and packing plants on the South Side. Soon after the butchering ended the bar opened for business. It must have been a big improvement not to taste blood in the wind, blown over the city from the slaughterhouses. When I lived in Chicago, those old abattoirs, long ago lost to history, had become inviolate and fixed in legend, but the city was changing again.

It was destroying itself, or sloughing off its old industrial self, and many of the brick warehouses and factory buildings in the neighborhood, gutted and windowless, deserted, were no better than caves hollowed from rock, with doors gaping open blackly, home to the homeless, the vast vacant interiors lit only by the light of fires burning in oil drums. In seeking the future, a city like Chicago wrecks itself and returns to stone, at least briefly. There were piles of rubble such as you imagine in war, but the absence of declared enemies, and the lethargic unfolding of time, its leisurely pace, kept people from seeing the scale of the shift as catastrophic. Factories and warehouses and hotels, these old muscular hopes came down in heaps of brick and mortar, of pulverized concrete and cracked limestone, and then those cairns of rock, in turn, were cleared off to reveal barren lots as flat and featureless as the prairie they'd supplanted. Now brand new buildings staunchly occupy those spaces, but for the duration, for the brief winter, spring and summer I lived and worked next door to the bar, there was the constant gray taste of mortar on my tongue, my lips burning from the lime that laced it, as clouds of dust were set adrift by each new day's demolition.

Dry, dusty, a desert, a war—another way to think about brick is that it's relocated earth, and that the streets of a city like Chicago recreate a riverbank, in this case the clay banks of the Mississippi and Ohio Rivers, where a good portion of Chicago's brick originally came from. The mining of clay is often referred to as "winning," a curious kind of victory considering the clay used in brickmaking comes from the Carbon-iferous period, a subcategory of the Paleozoic, some 340 million years ago. Such a vast span of time would seem to temper any man's sense of triumph. It was during the Carboniferous that amniotic eggs allowed ancestral birds, mammals and reptiles to reproduce on land; flight was first achieved, too, as insects evolved wings. And then something happened, something happened to the birds and mammals and reptiles, to the nascent flying insects, to the whole ambition and direction of that geologic age. Everything died off and disappeared in that silent way only an eon can absorb and keep secret.

And yet with death the seedless vascular plants that existed in tropical swamp forests provided the organic material that became coal. These dead plants didn't completely decay and instead turned to peat bogs. When the sea covered the swamps, marine sediments covered the peat, and eventually intense pressure and heat transformed these organic remains into coal and shale. Curiously, burning brick in kilns only extends and completes the process epochal time itself used to form the source clay. Brick manufacturers use coal to fire and harden the clay, removing moisture and the last memory, the last vestiges of fluidity from the brick. (In fact there's a taxonomy of bricks based on how burnt they are: clinker brick, nearest the fire, becomes vitrified, glassy and brittle; red brick is the hardest and most desirable product of the kiln; and salmon brick, sitting farthest from the fire, is underburned and soft, unsuitable for exposed surfaces.) The obvious advantage of brick as a building material is that it's already burned, which accounts for its presence in Chicago after the fire of 1871. Brick transformed the city, ushering in an era of industrial greatness, completing—no, not completing, but extending, extending a process that began with a mysterious extinction, a vast unimagined loss, a long time ago.

During my time in Chicago my day job was to load cars and trucks with reproduction furniture, the historical imperative of which had vanished, vaguely, around the turn of the century. Nonetheless shoppers from the suburbs drove to the city to browse the warehouse, its four floors and forty thousand square feet of fake antiques. They bought oxblood leather wingbacks, banker's lamps, baker's racks, oak iceboxes, old phones with a crank on the side that would, with a turn or two, summon the operator. The furniture was hokey, farmy, depressiony. Of course none of the people who shopped the warehouse were cutting blocks of winter ice to haul by horse and wagon and then pack and preserve in layers of straw for the long hot summer. They lived in the suburbs, they had appliances. It was curious and teleologically baffling. Why buy a phone you have to crank by hand when you

can punch buttons to place your call? Why a wrought-iron baker's rack for men and women whose cookies and bread did their cooling at the factory? Why buy an antique that was hardly two weeks old?

The chaotic layout of the warehouse led many customers to believe they might, in some obscure corner, find a rare treasure overlooked by others. But all this old stuff was absolutely brand new; we carried special crayons in our pockets to keep it that way, coloring in the scratches before we showed people their purchases. These people wanted old furniture but perfect, they wanted antiques without time (the main ingredient and, you'd think, the very source of value in anything vintage). Still, the animating urge, the desire for the real wasn't dead; the day I started the job I noticed nobody bought from the top, no one purchased the front item. Looking behind, for these people, equaled searching for the past, the authentic. Picky, savvy shoppers always made their selections by searching deep into the stacks and piles, mistrusting the surface, the present appearance of things, seeking the ideal, way back behind—behind what?

Maybe nostalgia is a species of the ideal, a dream of a last interior, where all the commotion of a life is finally rewarded with rest, drained of history. We were selling the memory of something, of hard work and industry, of necessity, of craft and artisanship—the mendacious

idea that life was gathered with greater force and organized in superior ways in the past. These faux antiques replaced the real past with an emblematic one. Or something. I could never quite untwist the riddle completely. When you stood in the warehouse the eye was pleasantly bombarded by a vastness filled. But the inspiration for most of the furniture we sold came originally from hardscrabble times, times of scarcity and unrest and an economy based on need, not surplus, and certainly not this absurd superfluity, this crazy proliferation, where two hundred oak iceboxes, stacked to the ceiling on layers of cardboard, would easily sell out on a Saturday afternoon. Why were people so avid and enthusiastic for the emblems of hardship? For what idealized interior could this possibly serve as honest décor?

After closing I'd slip a padlock in the loading dock door, then stay inside: the furniture warehouse was also my home, I lived in there, vaguely employed as a night watchman. Every night I slept on one of, I'm guessing, two hundred sofas. I ate takeout dinners on tables that would be sold the next day. I read books by the greenish light of an ugly banker's lamp, set on a fake oak icebox. My boss was a man of great good fortune who liked to squire his mistress around town in a restored Model-T Ford. He hired me to deter theft, set out glue traps and hose down the dump-

sters so bums wouldn't light the cardboard on fire, trying to keep warm. I simplified my job by rigging a cheap alarm system out of magnetic triggers and a hundred yards of lampwire and a couple Radio Shack sirens perched on the windowsills. In the evenings I'd arm the thing by twisting together the exposed copper strands and head next door to my uncle's bar.

You entered the bar through a black door with a diamond peephole. There were nine stools covered in red leatherette. My uncle did book and collected numbers. Among the patrons you found a deep well of faith, a certain gut feel for what Catholic theologians would call analogical thinking, whereby you come to know the reality of God through signs. Gambling was how you negotiated the tricky path between situation and symbol. Winning was always an answer to a question. Most of the men were spooky about the stool they sat on and would rather stand all night than take a seat that had somehow been hoodooed by past bad luck. Many of these gamblers were afraid of the past, haunted by it, and this tilted their faith in the direction of fate, a less ample, less accommodating idea. On any given night thousands of bloated dollars would sit on the bar in wet frowning stacks. I'd never seen such sums. I drank Old Style and peppermint schnapps and lived off pork rinds and pickled eggs. The eggs floated in a gallon jar of green, amniotic pond-water-like specimens of some kind of nascent life form. The first bite of one was an act of courage.

Gambling and dim light and slow rising smoke and the forgottenness of the place made it seem like everybody in the bar had strange and compelling mysteries behind them. They were dense with background, or so you inferred, or romanticized, because the present, the very surface of life, was so meager, so without evidence or account. In this sense my take on these men wasn't all that different from the way the warehouse customers saw our fake antiques. Any "background" I granted them was just another kind of décor, the décor of history, of image—in particular history and image in their arrested or hardened forms, as nostalgia and cliché. The bar was the kind of place where people were "characters" and were known, to the extent that they were known at all, by some fragment of personality, a piece of self broken off and magnified until it was more recognizable than the original man behind it, overshadowing him. Character, in the bar, really was fate.

And so a character named Red Devil seemed a proxy voice, speaking for everybody, when he would cackle hysterically and yell out, "Manteno, 1963. I'm history!" Manteno was the state psychiatric hospital but nothing beyond that was elaborated. To be history in America doesn't mean to be recorded, noted, added to the narrative, but precisely the opposite, to be gone, banished, left behind. To be history is to be cut from the story.

Other characters? Here are two. They even have character names, names I'd avoid if I were writing fiction: Al and George.

Al tended the bar at night. He'd been in the Merchant Marine and ate with a fat clunky thumb holding down his plate as if he were afraid the whole place might pitch and yaw and send his dinner flying. He was dwarfish and looked like an abandoned sculpture, a forgotten intention. His upper body was a slab-like mass, a plinth upon which his head rested; he had a chiseled nose and jaw, a hackjob scar of a mouth; his hands were thick and stubby, more like paws than anything prehensile. Sitting back behind the bar, smoking Pall Malls, he seemed petrified, the current shape of his body achieved by erosion, his face cut by clumsy strokes and blows. His eyes, though, were soft and blue, always wet and weepy with rheum, and when you looked at Al, you had the disorienting sense of something trapped, something fluid and human caught inside the gray stone vessel of his gargoyle body, gazing out through those eyes. He was my only real neighbor. At closing he'd collect the glasses, wipe down the bottles, shut the blinds and go to sleep on the bar. In the morning he'd fold his blankets and stow them away in a cardboard box.

George was another fixture in the bar, a salesman working, like me, in the furniture warehouse. He drank beer all day, chased with shots of peppermint schnapps so that his breath would smell fresh, as though he'd just brushed his teeth. Like most drunks he had the baffling notion he was getting away with it, fooling everybody. I felt sorry for George because he wasn't fooling anybody and couldn't see the truth, that he was being tolerated and temporarily ignored. With his insulin shots, instant coffee, his shabby dress, his elaborate comb-over, he led an obscure life, irregular and unobserved, except at the bar. There he gambled with a nervousness torqued up tight by a belief in the quick tidy fate of accidents, of moments that decide everything. Some time in the past, he believed, things had gone wrong, gone fatally so. The present was his evidence. Divorce. Bankruptcy. Alcoholism. He had a gimpy leg, he was diabetic. He gambled the games, the horses, the numbers, the state lottery, everything. Sometime in the future there was a wager that would be won, a score that would redress everything, and perhaps this injection of faith, more than, say, a visit to the doctor, eased the pain for him.

"When I have money," he told me, "I can't sleep, I can't hardly eat. I don't feel good until it's gone."

In the bar a small bet was called "an interest bet," a wager that attached you fiercely, with greater vividness, to the flow of an otherwise monotonous day. It offered you a way into time, via the wide and democratic avenue of chance; even the smallest gamble instantly gave you a stake in the outcome of time itself. With a bet on, time had something to show you, held the promise of a revelation. When George was betting he had the sensibility of a psychotic, or a poet. There were nuances to assay, meanings to consider. Accidents became auguries. The odds on unrelated matters changed. Emotions rose to the surface, the buried inner life became relevant, and he grew sensitive, tender, his instinctual self, now resuscitated, engaged in the world's new density. Nothing out in the actual world demanded quite the same concentration of being, the same focused energy. With money on the line, he became aware of time, his place in it, and planned ahead. On payday he broke half his check into quarters, dimes and nickels, storing the coins in a coffee can at home; it was the only way he could keep himself from gambling all his money and make sure he'd have enough saved aside for food at the end of the month.

Every week I went to the Art Institute to look at Van Gogh's painting of his bedroom in Arles. Van Gogh's bedroom seemed an oasis, every bit as paradisal as the work of Gauguin, with exotic colors in thick impasto that in fact resemble his friend's Tahitian scenes. The painting offers a vision of an idealized interior space, one that meant something to me at a time when I was living in a furniture warehouse, amid such a wild, absurd, insane proliferation. By contrast, Van Gogh's room is simple. There's nothing tawdry or cheap, no excess, just what's needed—and need itself feels like a known quantity. Everything in the picture exists in pairs, two chairs, two bottles, the shutters, the pillows, and even though the room is empty, you feel desire in the quiet pairings, you anticipate a match, a union. The mirror above the washbasin is blank but the portraits on the walls speak and seem to people the solitude. The mood is secure and wishful: the room looks both inhabited and somehow waiting for an arrival. There's a chair angled by the bed, near the head of it, next to the pillows, as if a conversation had recently taken place, or would soon, between two people who understand one another. Everything is painted from your perspective, every line is arranged to invite you in. To your right you can see the door, so that's not where you're standing, like a stranger. You're already inside the room.

Van Gogh wrote of the work in a letter, saying that everything "is to be suggestive here of *rest* or of sleep in general," that the "picture ought to rest the brain, or rather the imagination," that it should express "inviolable rest."

Most people in the area around the bar were passing through, transient. They were commuters who caught the trains and left be-

hind an acute emptiness, a hollow around seven o'clock every night. Of course some people came in search of precisely this lacuna, this moment when the day lapsed into nothingness. Richard Speck sought it, holing up at the Starr Hotel a few blocks away, paying ninety cents a night for his furnished room, in the weeks after he'd murdered eight student nurses. This was 1966 and Speck planned to hop a freight train west but never managed to leave the Loop until he was sentenced to death. The single nurse who survived that attack, hidden flat beneath a bed, figured in my dreams for years. She squeezed herself beneath that bed and for hours listened to the sounds of sex followed by the sounds of death. I was a very young boy when this proto-horrific crime happened but for some reason I know Speck tenderly asked the last woman he was raping if she'd wrap her legs around him. That winter they tore down the Starr Hotel and I watched from a distance, watched the swing of a wrecking ball as it arced through the air, collided soundlessly, then came through, a couple seconds later, with a laggard explosion of crumbling brick.

At night black men in jalopy flatbeds scavenged through mounds of debris to save the bricks. In a book about brick, D. Knickerbacker Boyd writes: "When two bricks are struck together, they should emit a metallic ring." That's true. Bricks clink together with a satisfying ring akin to fine crystal.

The sound has a clarity, a rightness. Bricks also improve with age; highly valued skids of cured Chicago brick were sold to people as far away as Phoenix and San Francisco, people who made walkways, garden walls and barbecues from remnants of old factories. At night the air cleared of dust. To the west was Greek Town, across the freeway, with a row of restaurants concentrated enough so that some nights I'd pick up the arid scent of ore-gano; north was the Haymarket with its rotting fruit and from somewhere, on certain nights, in a building I searched for but could never locate, a candy maker spread the smell of chocolate and cinnamon in the air. From my window in the warehouse I'd hear the black men knocking away like moonlighting archaeologists, knocking until the old soft mortar was chipped loose and the clean red brick rang out as resonantly as a bell.

In the bar people kept drinking and betting right up to the very end. One night a stranger appeared and took George by the arm and led him gently, like a church usher, out to the sidewalk. Words were exchanged in pantomime. After a minute the stranger crushed George in the head with a length of pipe. George had raised his arms in supplication, beseeching, and when the pipe crashed down, his head bowed penitentially before he slumped to his knees, then fell forward on his face. You hardly ever see adults on the ground, they don't spin or twirl, they don't flop over and fall

for the fun of it, not like kids. In my experience adults only went to the ground in death. George owed the man money. It was a confusing sight, seeing him like that, a grown man sprawled out on the sidewalk, small and broken, with no more control over himself than a child.

Now when I think of it, I understand it was never so much the potential for gain that animated gamblers like George, these men who had nothing, but being reawakened to a world where loss was once again possible. That's really what gave them life and drove them again and again to the game. Loss was their métier and to have that taken away, to be, finally, lost, was the worst thing imaginable. As long as you could fall farther you distinguished yourself from the fallen. Loss reinstated possibility, but possibility without hope. And perhaps this explains how all of us blithely imagined that the general wreckage would pass over the bar, that it was somehow exempt. Gambling offered a re-fuge from the outside world, its advances, its mysterious evolution. No one believed the bar would end, not because we didn't believe in progress, but instead, more precisely, because our kind of gambling, the wish of it, was an attempt to salvage the past. We weren't so much hoping to change the future as we were trying to amend history. We wanted the past completely restored and made livable. We believed that was the only kind of winning that counted.

EXCESSIVELY SO:

PHOTOGRAPHS Derry Moore
ORIGINAL TEXT David Mlinaric

In his text, David Mlinaric made the case for a specific Rothschild approach to decorating with French furnishings—one that did not come naturally to an Englishman. It took years of working on the restoration of Waddesdon (pronounced "Waddsden") Manor to teach Mlinaric that in such a milieu "le superflu est nécessaire." Here, great richness has been harmonized so that it no longer overwhelms. *This page:* The Red Drawing Room in 1994, before its redecoration. *Opposite page:* The Red Drawing Room redecorated (with, among other things, Gainsborough's portrait from 1782 of a still slender Prince of Wales). Backgrounds for these pages were taken from Jennifer Bartlett's *Houses: Thin Lines*, oil on canvas (1997-98). *Following page (left):* A lesser guest room. It absorbs a few high-style French pieces into an intimate Victorian setting.

THE ROTHSCHILDS AT WADDESDON MANOR

SUBSCRIBE

www.nestmagazine.com

1-888-321-nest

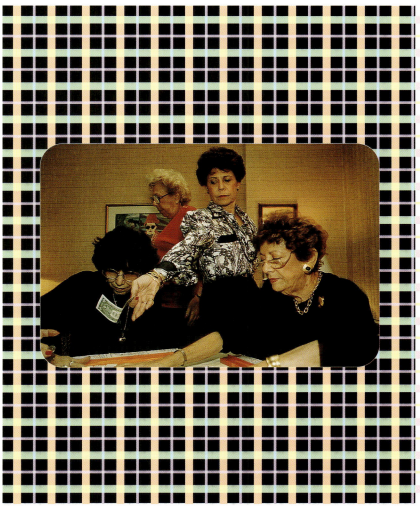

BE GENEROUS

nest GIFT SUBSCRIPTIONS

www.nestmagazine.com

1-888-321-nest

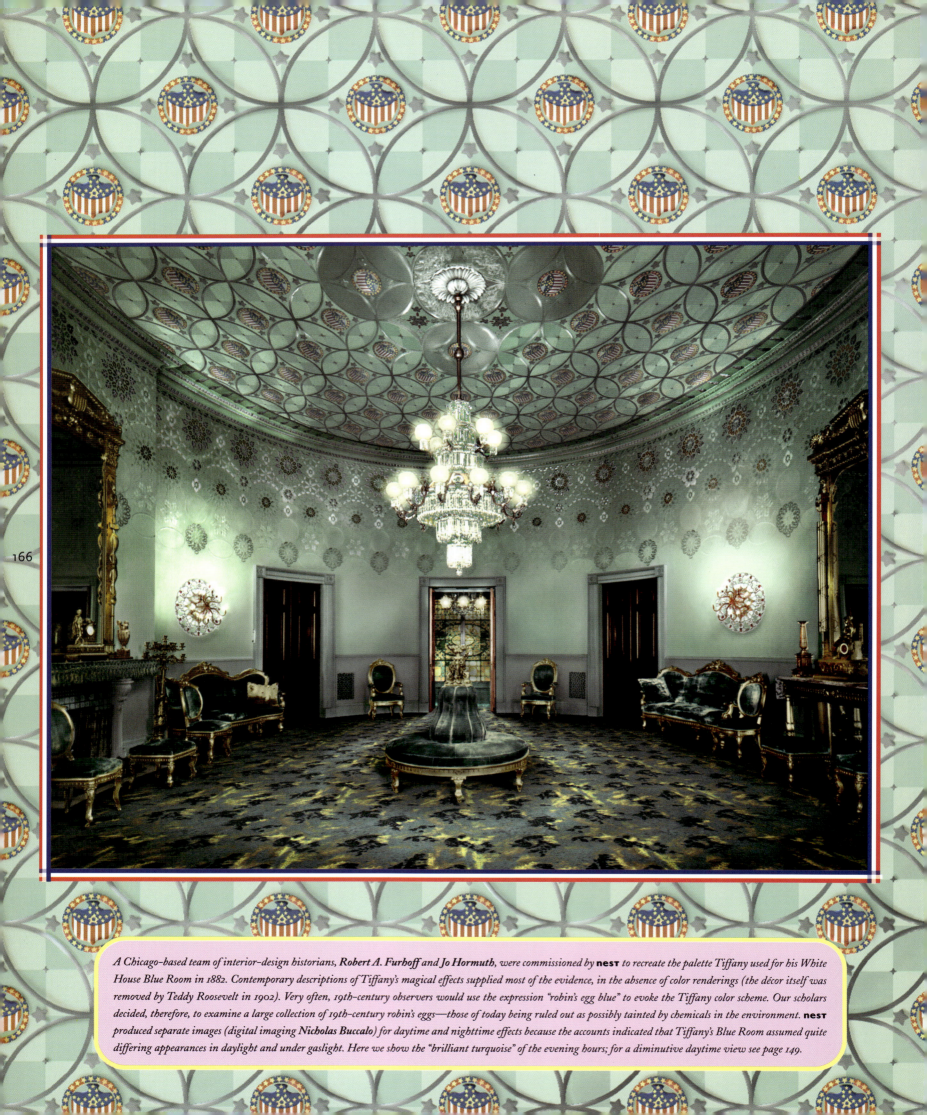

166

*A Chicago-based team of interior-design historians, **Robert A. Furhoff** and **Jo Hormuth**, were commissioned by **nest** to recreate the palette Tiffany used for his White House Blue Room in 1882. Contemporary descriptions of Tiffany's magical effects supplied most of the evidence, in the absence of color renderings (the décor itself was removed by Teddy Roosevelt in 1902). Very often, 19th-century observers would use the expression "robin's egg blue" to evoke the Tiffany color scheme. Our scholars decided, therefore, to examine a large collection of 19th-century robin's eggs—those of today being ruled out as possibly tainted by chemicals in the environment. **nest** produced separate images (digital imaging **Nicholas Buccalo**) for daytime and nighttime effects because the accounts indicated that Tiffany's Blue Room assumed quite differing appearances in daylight and under gaslight. Here we show the "brilliant turquoise" of the evening hours; for a diminutive daytime view see page 149.*

Letting toilet seats slam is one thing not to do while on board a Trident sub, **nest** learned (enemy sonar might hear you). Still, the experienced teams who man these vessels for months at a time do not always have to keep the lid on frustrations. In fact, they can even have fun. Or so our writer, **Chuck Palahniuk**, claimed. Our photographer, **Amy Eckert**, provided the woman's point of view on this impressive expanse of virile paraphernalia.

ADULT BABY

PHOTOGRAPHS **MITCH EPSTIEN**
ORIGINAL TEXT **KIERA COFFEE**

Daybee, our adult baby, in his home nursery, which he kept locked while out. He constructed this robust crib (6' high, 4'3" wide, and 7'8" long) in his free time in order to live out fantasies of becoming a pre–toilet-trained toddler again. Every night he was home Daybee would sleep in the crib. (There was room in it for others who shared his fetish and were willing to role-play his caretaker.) After he came out to her in 1998, Daybee's sister began sewing adult-size baby clothes for him; she then developed her own online business to meet the special clothing needs of the AB market.

SPECIAL EMBASSY

How time flies! Once again a dull sun was hugging the horizon, and in our vicinity darkness came crowding halfway between lunch and dinner. In other words, that revamped Saturnalia, Christmas, was not far off. Determined as always to put the best face on things, we laser-blasted a small equilateral cross through **nest** 11 (winter 2000-2001) from front to back. It was placed dead center, and every page in the issue had to cope. One byproduct of the laser process was singeing—differing with the various grades of paper and not entirely controllable—a welcome whiff of trouble in an overly complacent world.

The spirit of the season animated "Dear Mr. Lauren," our up front topic, for which **nest** editor-in-chief smuggled a photographer into the flagship Madison Avenue establishment, along with himself. If Mr. Polo wouldn't advertise with us, we'd still advertise with him. This was sort of a gift to ourselves, courtesy of a third party. Reluctant clerks were told that photos of Holtzman trying on suits were needed for his mother (it being no easy matter to decide on the perfect suit for an invalid aunt's 80th-birthday fiesta in Palm Beach).

nest's visit to Pololand was heralded by the editor's letter, which took the form of a modest proposal. After setting out our bedrock rule of not smuggling plugs for advertisers into features and professing pride in our "virginal editorial pages," we hinted at our readiness to "loosen up" for a Polo ad. Under the cloak of satire, Holtzman was addressing an unsavory magazine industry practice that is taken for granted nowadays. A serious piece on the taste Lauren so successfully promotes, in part through his highly decorated stores, came with the issue as well ("Polo, Anyone?").

The features in issue 11 were perhaps even more diverse than usual. Andrée Putman was here, in her own words ("Andrée Putman by Herself"), but so, too, was the community house of the Amazonian Matis, its ambiance evoked by a French anthropologist who enjoys most-favored-foreigner status among this small group deep in the Brazilian jungle. "Still Waters" paid mega tribute to filmmaker John Waters, who has done more for bad taste than anyone else we know. (His home was a surprise.) "Doomsday Rooms" told of the enormous bomb shelter secretly readied for Congress by the United States government in the early 1960s; "Napoleon's Penis" (the "final **nest**" for issue 11) paid elaborate tribute to a sovereign relic with the aid of some ten thousand Italian honeybees.

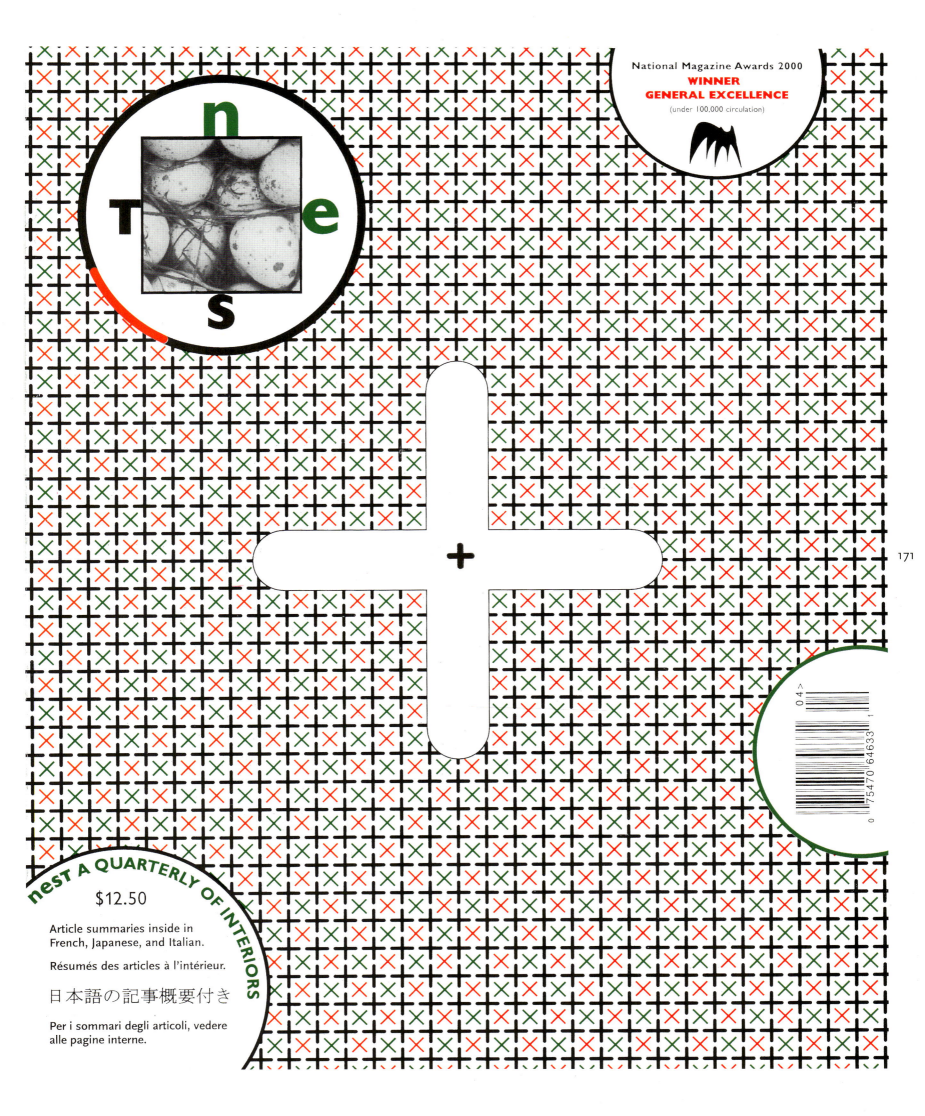

n
e
T
S

171

nEST A QUARTERLY OF INTERIORS

$12.50

Article summaries inside in
French, Japanese, and Italian.

Résumés des articles à l'intérieur.

日本語の記事概要付き

Per i sommari degli articoli, vedere
alle pagine interne.

0 4 >

0 75470 64633 1

Dear Mr. Lauren:

Looking out my window I see your flagship store, only a stone's throw down Madison. How sad you and I are not closer in other ways, too.

Sometime we ought to get together and talk about why you've never joined the **nest** family. Has there been a misunderstanding? Granted, our virgin editorial pages *are* a source of pride. Still I might loosen up to get a Polo ad. They tell me everybody does.

I'm cooking right now. For instance, Borneo. Why not do another tropical treehouse, I'm thinking, and put them all in Polo shirts? Or forget the exotic locale. It would be a cinch to shoot one of our sentimental homeless-at-Christmas features in front of your windows. Once you get the basic idea, the possibilities are endless!

Maybe someone's already done it, but there could even be a little formula, like 1ED = 1AD, where I give you one page of editorial and you buy one ad page in exchange. It would prevent confusion, and think of the savings on lunch.

I'll probably drop over one of these days, since waiting for a formal invitation from anyone can be a mistake. Anyway, a favorite aunt of mine is about to have her eightieth birthday, and I want to surprise her with one of your nice conservative suits. To really give her a thrill, you know?

Look forward to seeing you.

Yours sincerely,

P.S. Be sure not to miss "Polo, Anyone?", another feature of special interest to you in this issue.

172

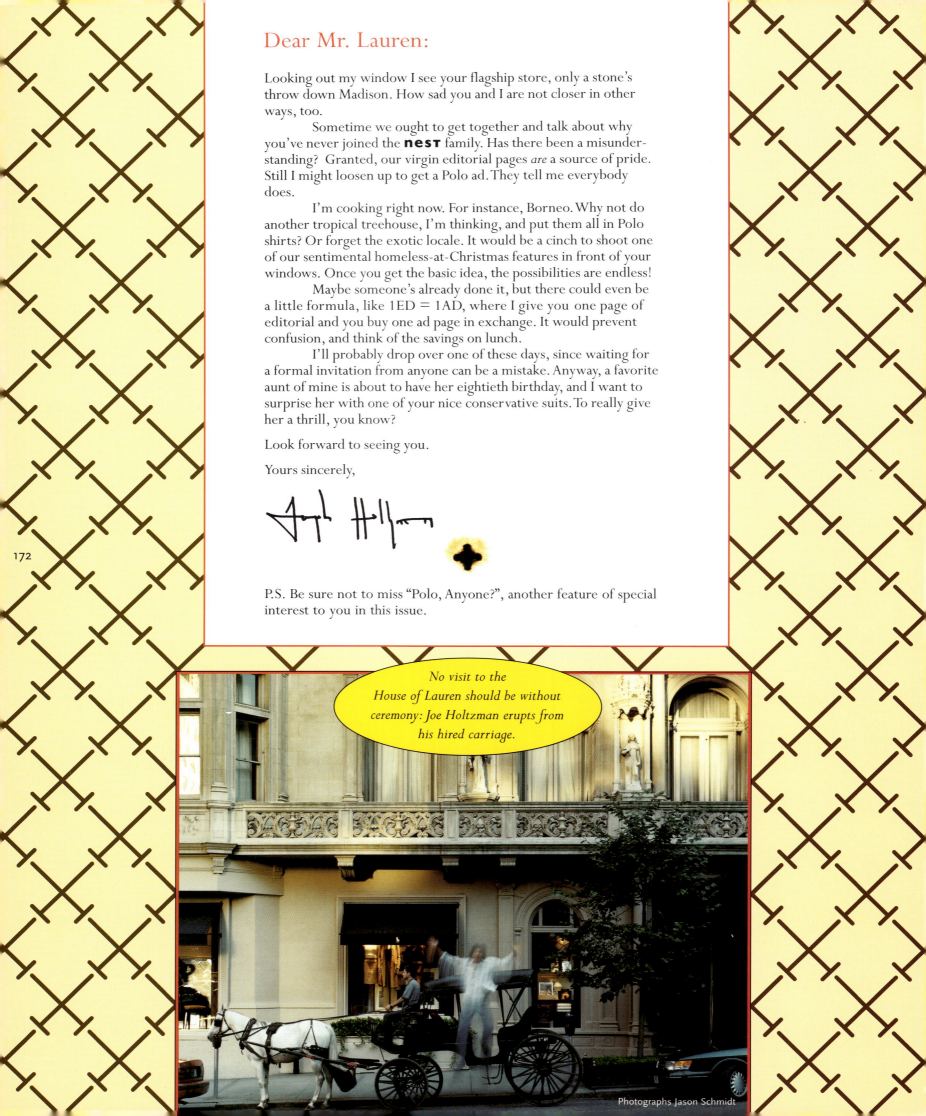

No visit to the House of Lauren should be without ceremony: Joe Holtzman erupts from his hired carriage.

Photographs Jason Schmidt

173

Here's to us, Ralph.

photos Jason Schmidt

Above:
Holtzman spreading cheer in
The Home Collection.

Above:
Keeping warm by
the fire.

Above:
Raising suspicions in Classics
for Her.

Above: Phoning
Hong Kong on the House
line is cheaper.

A little more
exposure on Madison Avenue,
for a good cause.

nest

ANDRÉE PUTMAN BY HERSELF

PHOTOGRAPHS **CATHERINE OPIE** & **DAPHNE FITZPATRICK**
ORIGINAL TEXT **ANDRÉE PUTMAN**

177

Opposite page: On the back cover of **nest** 11 Andrée Putman seemed to wear a brooch in the bold Putman taste, in consequence of her laser cross being set off by a white circle. The eminent decorator penned her own text for our feature on her Paris apartment ("Andrée Putman by Herself"). This iconic space had been featured in many other magazines, but we gave it unprecedented coverage (with images by Catherine Opie and Daphne Fitzpatrick). *This page:* Putman's bedroom alcove lies just off her main room. Despite sliding glass panels veiled with mosquito netting, her sleeping quarters did not seem at all secluded. Perhaps the whole loft is a zone of privacy which needs no enhancing. *Following two pages:* One of several views we offered of Putman's main room. The steel dining room chairs to the left were designed by Ruhlmann and fabricated by Brandt in 1932. The Milky Way rug behind Putman is of her own design; the other round rug (left) was created by Eileen Gray.

UPSTREAM LIVING

PHOTOGRAPHS **Nicolas Reynard**   ORIGINAL TEXT **Philippe Erikson**

Both the photographer and **nest** fancied the orange discoloration along the margins of this photograph of the exterior of the Matis longhouse (which 18th-century Europeans compared to an inverted ship's hull). Our text, concerned with what went on inside, dwelt on the peculiar character of social space there. "For nearly fifteen years now," Philippe Erikson's narrative commenced, "I have been spending time with the Matis. And for more than ten, Kwini has been calling me *kaniwa kimo,* 'true cross-cousin,' rather than *nawa,* 'foreigner.' I have returned so often to this isolated spot, deep inside the Brazilian Amazon, that I no longer notice the body decorations, spectacular though they are, that enhance people's faces here. That their faces look feline strikes me less than the fact that there are now a few lines on Kwini's face or that his mother Shari's hair is turning gray. One thing, however, will always impress me and take my breath away whenever I return after a long absence: the vibrant atmosphere of the *shobo,* the communal house that Kwini shares with his two wives, their children, and about fifty other Matis. The mood is both serene and joyful, combining formality and restfulness and brightening each of my stays in that longhouse with a view, at the top of a hill, on the banks of the Rio Itui, several days away by boat from the nearest telephone."

DOOMSDAY ROOMS

PHOTOGRAPHS RICHARD BARNES

ORIGINAL TEXT TOM VANDERBILT

Every page of "Doomsday Rooms" converted its laser cross into the cross hairs of a target, an apt simile for our subject. The blast door shown here was concealed behind sliding panels for 30 years. Greenbrier Hotel guests would routinely pass it on their way to an Exhibit Center (down the hallway to the right), which was actually an integral part of the secret bunker.

STILL WATERS

PHOTOGRAPHS RICHARD BARNES
ORIGINAL TEXT BRENDA RICHARDSON

nest was the first ever to feature the Baltimore home of John Waters, and its tasteful trappings must have surprised some readers. But why, we thought, shouldn't a counterculture icon make himself comfy at home? At least there were occasional mementos from the films. In his front hall, for instance, the electric chair which enjoyed a spectacular bit part in *Female Trouble* (1974) blended with contemporary art (right wall, George Stoll's *Untitled (Ivory)*, 1997; left wall, Catherine Opie's photograph *House #3 (Beverley Hills)*, 1995). *Opposite page:* **nest** also published 100 images from John Water's Polaroid diary: Since 1992 the director has been documenting everyone who comes through the front door of the house, except for members of his staff.

PAT MORAN
GREER YEATON

3/19/92   LUNCH

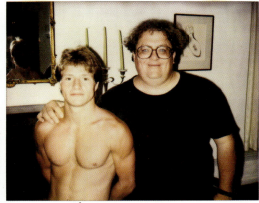

"KEITH" 8/10/92
AND BOB ADAMS   A VISIT

7/3/94   before
RICKIE + ROB   dinner

3/23/92   ROSA GRIFFITH   WORK

8/20/92   WEEKEND
Henry Garfinkel   hous*guest

12/13/94   Coffee
JOE HOLZMAN

5/2/92   POST-
Jeffrey Pratt Gordon   CLUB CHARLES

2/11/93   TAX
PAUL YANCHUS   ACCOUNTANT

6/10/87   dinner
Dad + Mom

7/31   Dennis Dermody   WEEKEND
HOUSE
GUEST

4/5/94   "ENTERTAINMENT
Mink Stole, Patty Hearst   Tonite"
SHOOT

7/12   NEST photo shoot
Brenda Richardson, Brady Lee,   Richard
BARNES

final **nest**

NAPOLEON'S

PENIS

PHOTOGRAPHS JAMES WOJCIK

ORIGINAL TEXT PAUL B. FRANKLIN

In tracing the postmortem history of Napoleon's penis, Paul B. Franklin introduced a cast of entertaining characters. Chief among them was Dr. John K. Lattimer, former chairman of the Department of Urology of Columbia Medical School who had become custodian of the imperial member in 1978. *"As a matter of policy,"* the octogenarian collector cautioned **nest**, *"we have never permitted his actual specimen to be photographed . . . even in this* 'Clintonian' era." Yet he allowed the black leather box in which it was supposed to slumber to be photographed, amid a swarm of bees. Our fey notion was to create a contemporary reliquary out of a cloud of guardian bees, since these creatures had served as Napoleon's decorative emblem in life. Below: **nest** took readers behind the scenes to recount its adventure with the bees. Few stories exact such physical pain as this one did.

DECORATORS BORN

The last issue in our even **nest** dozen (spring 2001) turned its attention to the D-gene, rumored to be responsible for that irrepressible interest in decorating shown by certain individuals from their earliest years. "Genetic Decorator," the up front story, recorded an experiment in which a 6-year-old suspected by **nest** of being one was encouraged to redecorate his bedroom. For this exercise a professional painter and seamstress were imported to do the child's bidding. And since dyed-in-the-wool decorators never worry about expenses, we saw no reason to let fall so much as a syllable about them.

Little Dan, duly pleased with himself, shared the front cover with his new jungle theme bedroom. Every decorating decision had been his alone, down to the rose-studded ribbon trim for a zebra chair. Although our editor-in-chief could not concur in all his choices, Dan had a mind of his own and manipulating him proved next to impossible. **nest** was on the trail of the D-gene for sure. Dan appeared again on the rear cover, with his major decorating faculties mapped for the benefit of researchers. Perhaps we hoped for a modest revival of the glorious 19th-century science of phrenology, to which the world is indebted for an immense body of observations on skull shape and its subtle connections with psychology.

One bird—the peacock—so fascinated our prodigy that **nest** decided to decorate the up front pages with peacock-inspired wallpapers, in homage to both bird and boy. No more peacocks were needed for "Julian Schnabel: Decorator," however, which proudly displayed the painter and filmmaker in a new role. Nor were there any in "So Many Tigers, So Little Time," a feature on Yoichi "Yogi" Nishikawa's Tokyo apartment, filled with tigers of every stripe.

In **nest** 12 we tried out several new pitches to attract subscribers. For one, readers were exposed to an honest explanation of the economic realities that make subscribers absolutely essential to the magazine's survival. In token of the utter seriousness of this message, the page on which it appeared went undecorated. (We believe in treating readers as intelligent parties to be kept in the know.) And then three pages were devoted to our "Why Get Dressed to Get **nest**?" subscription offer, aimed at the heedless urban young who persist in picking us up at the newsstand. These pages, each posing a naked subscriber in her or his generic starter apartment, referred readers back to the important message (reprinted on page 194).

By the time you read this page, three more issues of **nest** will have seen daylight, we hope. Where will the magazine have gone by then? What new directions are to be tried? Almost certainly these upcoming issues will emerge the way our first twelve did, as separate acts of creation, hence unpredictable. There is nothing to do but stay tuned and savor each surprise, along with us.

Background wallpapers courtesy Cooper-Hewitt, National Design Museum, Smithsonian Institution

in search of the decorator gene

nest A QUARTERLY OF INTERIORS

$12.50 SPRING 2001

11 >

0 75470 64633 1

Article summaries inside in
French, Japanese, and Italian.

Résumés des articles à l'intérieur.

日本語の記事概要付き

Per i sommari degli articoli,
vedere alle pagine interne.

Cover photographs Jason Schmidt

THE GENETIC DECORATOR

STORY P.3

ENLARGED INTERIOR VISUALIZATION

REFINED COLOR DISCRIMINATION

HYPER SURFACE SENSITIVITY

?

PERFECT PROPORTION

SWAG SAVVY

TOTAL PATTERN RECALL

FABRIC LUST

Dan's family, with interloper. From left to right: Max, 11; Christine, his mother; John, his father; Joseph Holtzman, 43 and a half; and Dan, 6. Neither his parents nor brother Max are fazed in the slightest to be living with a genetic decorator, if that is what little Polo-shirt-loving Dan really is.

Dan, what will it be? As the rest of us stand and wait, an admiring circle, the humdrum mall scene is transformed into a Renaissance tableau with our decorator-prodigy at its center.

Big, peaceable Pat O'Brien, the painter who was flown in to supply custom wall treatments for our young decorator, must listen while Dan points out some error in his work. Pat is projecting a peacock sketched by Dan onto the wall as a floor-to-ceiling figure.

Before and after: Dan's house, a stately Victorian built in 1861, as it actually looked for **NEST**'s visit (left) and as it would look if the tiny terror ever had his way. We were delighted with Dan's scheme: Curry Sauce for the clapboards, trim in Mystic Blue, and a Twig Basket front door.

IMPORTANT

If you bought this magazine from a newsstand, we lost money.

nest already costs a lot to make (you can tell), and when you add shipping, storage, and the newsstand's cut, the total comes out to about $15.50 a copy.

We'll never compromise our production standards, so there won't be any savings there. **nest** is, above all else, an object, and we couldn't stomach saddling the world with another poorly made object. Given our commitment to production standards far higher than those for most hardbound art books, a $12.50 cover price is as low as we can go (lower, actually).

However, there is another way to lower costs, and those of you who like the magazine can help–you can invest in **nest** by subscribing. Buying a **nest** subscription not only helps us keep the costs down by cutting out the newsstand, it generates income by enabling us to charge more for the select few ads we're willing to run.

With the stability and savings subscriptions bring us, we can charge you only $8.50/issue, and still clear enough profit to make the next one.

nest is that rare bird, the self-supporting independent magazine, and we want to stay that way. So please invest in the future of **nest** by subscribing.

Above: This message may have been a first in the magazine business. Using plain English, we shared privileged information with our readers to let them see how *they* could help *us*. We view readers as partners deserving an active role.

Opposite page: "Imposing Taste" revealed the underbelly of a celebrated house outside Paris. The high life went on here, come rain, come shine, come World War II and the Germans. While most of Paris went without, there was always more than enough to eat at Chateau de Groussay. It was a time when heirlooms were being bartered away by aristocrats for a chicken or two. Charles de Beistegui, Groussay's owner, possessed many chickens and refined if somewhat theatrical taste (this photo is of his double-story library). Clive Aslet, editor-in-chief of *Country Life*, told us the tale. Charlotte Whalen, of **nesт**'s graphics department, designed the tricolor typeface for the feature's title.

Photograph Sotheby's

IMPOSING TASTE

195

JULIAN SCHNABEL

nesт acclaimed Julian Schnabel as a master decorator in presenting his Montauk summer cottage, built by Stanford White in the "shingle style" in 1882. The painter and his wife, Olatz, undertook an imaginative restoration and made the place absolutely suit themselves in the bargain. Of our many features on artists' houses, only this one revealed the occupant as a full-fledged talent in **nesт**'s own department. *Following two pages:* Part of the trick for Schnabel was learning to domesticate his paintings in a house of such marked historical character. In the stairwell off the main entrance hall, for example, he sought to enhance White's paneling with some quite small paintings. Above was room for a towering vertical canvas, *Procession for Jean Virgo*, 1979. Schnabel, who did the photography for his feature assisted by a **nesт** regular, Andreas Pauly, placed these flowers on the rug.

DECORATOR

SO MANY TIGERS, SO LITTLE TIME

PHOTOGRAPHS YOSHIKO SEINO

ORIGINAL TEXT MARK ROBINSON

The year of the metal tiger comes only once in every 60. Yoichi "Yogi" Nishikawa, born in the year of the metal tiger, had become one himself—or so our caption ventured in accounting for the host of tiger objects he gathered into his Tokyo apartment. Tigers, "from the greatest and most ferocious to the cutest miniatures, keep watch with Nishikawa and guarantee that his fierce feline essence will never dissipate," it concluded. In here you found a life-size stuffed tiger toy made by Steiff, a tiger piano painted by Fabian Compton, a Garouste and Bonetti one-of-a-kind tiger bedroom ensemble, and countless pieces of tiger kitsch.

DEVIXIT
ANNO
MDCLIX

"Master Narrative" (reprinted here in full) gave second thought to a famous Baroque tomb towering inside Venice's Frari Church. Why, **nest** wondered, would four black giants have been enlisted to uphold forever Doge Giovanni Pesaro and his 90-foot pile of marble? The short answer was that these figures were Ottoman slaves and had symbolized Turkish subjection before the glory of Venice. A longer answer was suggested by *Carl Skoggard*'s text, which spoke the mind of an owner of human property roaming Western history from Homer onwards. At the same time, *Giorgio Jano*'s special camera showed the Pesaro tomb in a bent perspective stressing its four working figures at the expense of the Doge (perched way on high and out of sight, unless you counted a pair of cherubs hovering before the arms of his throne).

"WHO ARE YOU, WHERE DO YOU COME FROM?" WAS THE FIRST thing to ask of any stranger, from the disguised Odysseus returning home on down. Always these were the first questions asked—unless you arrived as a slave. Then we had none, and there were no dramatic possibilities. You'd lost your name, the use of a name; your precise birthplace no longer mattered. In fact, we felt it better not to know the old name. Soon enough you would have another to answer to.

Becoming one—a slave—was itself not so very odd. Everyone, even you, understood. By the time we laid eyes on you, the drama was over. Most likely you'd been captured in a faraway raid or skirmish that left no other trace. The circumstances meant little to us. One knew only that another stranger might have taken your life, and had spared it. That you had, at that moment, been reborn as a respectable item of exchange. The trade was a good one, going as far back as anyone could remember.

Very well, you had lost your life to another, and not altogether. Technically, you had been *reduced* to slavery. No doubt you kept the memory of just how it chanced to happen; a painful memory is preferable to having none. Yet we are to be forgiven, I suppose, for seeing only a common fate, repeated again and again. You were forever flocking here from every direction—speaking tongues we did not care to recognize, amusing us with your uncouth dress, your bizarre adornments. Our thought was to remedy such strangeness, and, frankly speaking, you were lucky to shed your ways for ours.

But we sensed more than simple bad luck in your affair. Evidently your gods, whoever they were, had abandoned you to calamity. It was idle to wonder just what you'd done or not done to propitiate them. Things between you had gone badly wrong; that was enough. Our gods, though, were pleased with the arrangement between you and us, a custom of the greatest antiquity belonging to the order of things. At the very least, we would give you exacting standards to live up to, something pleasing in the sight of any god.

The divinities with whom we dealt being satisfied with this arrangement, we expected our artists and wise men to second it. And so each did, offering us understanding in place of untutored conviction. Aeschylus saw in your enslavement the moving hand of fate; Sophocles, more penetrating perhaps, punishment for some fault or other. Plato was persuaded that the natural order demanded the subordination of inferiors; Aristotle did not disagree, but went on to devise a new category of living instruments, meant to put other instruments into motion. Your instrumentality was cherished by the best legal minds for the longest time.

Talk of your being an instrument, however, was not easy for many to grasp. For you reminded us of ourselves, reduction or no reduction. You tended to grow on one. Aristotle himself, always clever at distinctions, allowed that while we could never feel affection for you as a slave, we might befriend the human creature you also were. We felt relieved as well to have the Stoics. "The struggle against your chains is what truly makes you into slaves," they said. "Resign yourselves and you'll be free in spirit." Such doctrine helped you and us equally—for without pretending your lot was a happy one, we sought your contentment for our own happiness.

Looking back, I do not find it puzzling that you were among the first to seek out the Redeemer. Here at last was a religion tailor-made for the likes of you. For you certainly were sinners, as your condition attested, and you had so much less to give up. It was a giddy time; from every side arrived predictions of an imminent end. Fortunately, we were still hesitating about joining you and giving up all for Jesus when the new religion joined us instead as a proprietor in "this world." And presently we learned that the Lord God in Heaven, for reasons best known to Himself, had ordained your sort of property. St. Augustine spoke most clearly on the point in his *City of God*, which everybody went on reading for centuries.

We sometimes wondered, even with the good will of such authorities, what we held onto where you were concerned. It must have been an utterly simple thing. Perhaps the charm of the perpetual motion machine, translated into your flesh. Or perhaps merely the thrill of claiming absolute sway over a being not unlike oneself. Yet the irksome fact of you standing before us was far from simple. You were nothing like an implement. While none disputed our right to treat you as we chose, to inflict whatever punishment was appropriate for your shortcomings, it made no sense to injure our own property, to cause it to hate us.

But how tiresome always to be cajoling you to work for free! There is no denying we felt ourselves in something of a bind at times and nearly envied those who paid for servants. I will not mention your habit of running off, as if we hadn't anything better to do than track you down. As well, your wanting to marry was scarcely endearing, with all its unwelcome complications. Still more vexing were beddings we did not resist, the mingling of our blood. When things reached this pass, one might have no choice but to let you go. You'd made a mockery of the idea of reduction.

No matter, our arrangement would endure. You came and went, of course; we had our difficulties. But which social relation does not rely on compromise? Every so often, there was even an improvement to report. You will not have forgotten the quake of Islam slamming our world, with each religion supplying you to the other—surely a moral convenience for those who'd not reduce their own. And in truth, we always preferred that your reductions take place somewhere else. By this time you were really swarming, too, the Infidel being an indefatigable slaver, whatever else is said against him.

I have put off any mention of your contributions. By any measure they were impressive, even if you rarely exerted yourselves without encouragement. Whole empires rested on your labors in the kitchen, the bedroom, the schoolroom, the shop, the field, the mine. Irksome you might be, but we were loath to do without you. You built our roads and dredged our harbors. In a pinch, you fought our wars. You nursed us, wove our shrouds. You kept our accounts. You both dressed and undressed us. You made sure food was on the table, entertained us, perpetuated skills of every kind. You gave us leisure and also filled it. You made us feel good about ourselves. The list could go on, and don't think we lacked appreciation for what was owed you.

Now, we had never been ones to mind color, as you know; it was only a curious thing. You'd come in every hue. In these last years, however, you seemed to grow darker. You were the brilliant black flower of so many an Eastern train; our shores, too, saw you answer fashion and grow darker. Against shining silk, we all agreed, black was bewitching. And then, Africa was crossing the Atlantic. God's will would carry black people across the sea to slave for white and into the future as far as anyone could see: another world unimaginable without you.

Be that as it may, you loom before me here as upholders of the Doge. There can be no surprise finding you silently at work in this ancient sanctum. One cannot possibly object to your bare feet or torn leggings. Blankly clad, you preserve a fabulous dignity. Granted, the Turk himself should be bending underneath such a burden, but his slaves are far stronger and will not falter. No, sons of Ham, you are immensely strong, fit to bear anything. Your stature is unquestionable. You shall remain, I think, tenders of our glory forever.